Wagner's Ring
An introduction

Wagner's Ring
An Introduction

Alan Blyth

Hutchinson
London Melbourne Sydney Auckland Johannesburg

Hutchinson and Co. (Publishers) Ltd

An imprint of the Hutchinson Publishing Group

3 Fitzroy Square, London W1P 6JD

Hutchinson Group (Australia) Pty Ltd
30–32 Cremorne Street, Richmond South, Victoria 3121
PO Box 151, Broadway, New South Wales 2007

Hutchinson Group (NZ) Ltd
32–34 View Road, PO Box 40–086, Glenfield, Auckland 10

Hutchinson Group (SA) (Pty) Ltd
PO Box 337, Bergvlei 2012, South Africa

First published 1980

© Alan Blyth 1980

The material in the Discography first appeared in
Opera in Record, edited by Alan Blyth (Hutchinson, 1979)

Set in VIP Sabon

Printed in Great Britain by the Anchor Press Ltd
and bound by Wm Brendon & Son Ltd, both of Tiptree, Essex

ISBN 0 09 142011 3

Contents

Illustrations

All illustrations show the first Bayreuth production (1876)
and are reproduced by permission of the Bayreuth Festival

Foreword

Bernard Shaw in his 'Preliminary Encouragements' to *The Perfect Wagnerite* stated that '. . . *The Ring*, with all its gods and giants and dwarfs, its water-maidens and Valkyries, its wishing-cap, magic ring, enchanted sword, and miraculous treasure, is a drama of today, and not of a remote and fabulous antiquity'. That is as true now as it was when Shaw wrote it, nearly eighty years ago. His other dictum, on the music, also holds its validity: 'If the sound of music has any power to move them [those who are sceptical about understanding the work], they will find that Wagner exacts nothing further. There is not a single bar of "classical music" in *The Ring* – not a note in it that has any other point than the single direct point of giving musical expression to the drama'.

The Ring, for all its musical and dramatic complexity, does not need to be approached in awe. As Shaw implies, music and drama are as one and, once the text has been understood, the musical development falls naturally into place. In this volume, I want to show, as simply as possible, how the two correlate, and so enhance the experience, even – or perhaps particularly – for those who are hearing and seeing the work for the first time. To do that, it is necessary to approach the operas as far as possible from Wagner's point of view, so as to give a clear and unprejudiced view of the drama and music, and let the reader form his own opinion as to the 'meaning' of the whole. Most of those who have written about *The Ring*, from Shaw forward, have given their own interpretations of it, many of them revealing and instructive, but also controversial, and the virgin ear and eye will be unduly influenced by such views, if that is all that has been read. From a basic exposition, a newcomer can progress to absorbing personal views such as Shaw's and Robert Donington's, and each time he encounters the tetralogy he will see new facets, contemplate fresh ideas.

To understand Wagner the musician, we must be acquainted with Wagner the poet and Wagner the philosopher. Each complements the other, and we must try to discern what gave birth to a music-drama of such proportions, fifteen hours of music, of consecutive thought – by far the longest, most sustained, most ingenious ever attempted with success by any composer. As a work of art it demands a longer period of concentration than any other. The ideal place to hear it is Bayreuth, Wagner's own theatre, where the orchestra does not come between the singers and the audience and where the breaks between acts are long enough to allow for a mental and physical recharging of the batteries.

The creation of that theatre, and the first performance of the complete *Ring* there in 1876, a little over a hundred years ago, was the culmination of something that had formed but vaguely in the composer's mind some thirty years earlier, arising from his studies of Norse mythology. By 1848, at the comparatively early age of thirty-five, he was ready to write a complete prose sketch, a synopsis if you like, entitled *The Nibelung Saga as a Scheme for Drama*, drawing from the myths that which he considered of lasting significance. This synopsis was to undergo countless changes before it developed into the finished libretti for the operas as we know them today, but in essentials the scheme did not alter greatly, although the all-important forswearing of love by Alberich had still to be incorporated.

Wagner made a fair copy of this first plan between 4 and 8 October 1848, and then immediately went on to write the scenario for the first opera he had definitely in mind, *Siegfried's Death*; he completed that by the end of the following February. It was to end with the triumph of the gods through Siegfried's good works, a very different conclusion from the end of *Götterdämmerung* as that was finally conceived many years later. The conflict for final power between gods, giants and the subterranean creatures called Nibelungs (those who live in the mists) was thus to end in an apparent victory for the forces of good. Already in the later part of 1859 Wagner had second thoughts. After a re-reading of one of the old stories he realized that the gods must go down with the rest so that a new order could come to pass.

Wagner did not conceive his first musical thoughts for this work until 1850. How well prepared was he by then for what was to be such an immense undertaking? He had already written six operas. Although there is an enormous musical development between *Die Feen* (The Fairies) of 1833 and *Lohengrin* of 1848, he was himself dissatisfied with what he had achieved to date. Indeed, he seemed resolved to write no more operas, certainly not ones following the conventional mould of the first half of the nineteenth century. By 1850 his musical progress was just about advanced enough for him to tackle the vast project in his mind, if not to set it into its final form. Impecunious and seemingly unwanted as he then was, he had sufficient confidence in himself to proceed with his new ideas, propounding them in his own writings such as *Opera and Drama* (1850–51). Liszt befriended him at this time in Weimar, and got a commission for him to write *Siegfried's Death*.

Above all, Wagner was developing in his mind, consciously or subconsciously, one of the most revolutionary and significant ideas embodied in *The Ring*. Any newcomer to the work must realize that one of the essentials of *The Ring* is an unbroken continuity of musical construction, no longer allowing for conventional, formal numbers that delay the action. Music and play must go forward at one and the same time. That is why it was important for Wagner to be at once the poet and the composer of the work so that the music could develop hand in hand with the drama. All the time he was working on *Siegfried's Death*, the preliminary ideas, or at least the mood for the music, must have been going through his mind as he wrote the words. Indeed, musical thoughts fill the margins of the prose sketches.

By 1851, he already knew that *Siegfried's Death* could not stand on its own. He wrote to the conductor Hans von Bülow: 'I have greatly expanded my plan. *Siegfried's Death* is at present unproduceable and, for the public, incomprehensible; so I am going to preface it with a Young Siegfried'. He prepared the text of this during the spring of 1851. *Young Siegfried* and *Siegfried's Death*, taken as a whole, might well have formed a neater, more unified work, easier to understand, than *The Ring* as we now have it, but Wagner began to feel that he had something of much greater substance within his grasp. He decided to draw about 120 lines from Brünnhilde's Narrative in *Young Siegfried* and expand them into an individual work, *Die Walküre*, itself to be preceded by a Prelude, *Das Rheingold*. Having in the first place seen that the epic of *Siegfried's Death* needed to be prefaced by the more human *Young Siegfried*, he now perceived that he could not cram into that work all the material he needed to fulfil his grand design or to gain the understanding of future audiences.

In November 1851 Wagner drafted a first scenario for *Das Rheingold*, projected in three acts, with the title *The Rape of the Rheingold*. Then came a tentative sketch for *Die Walküre*, or at least two acts of it. In the subsequent year, both underwent drastic revision as he wrote their actual texts, his concept of the characters ever changing as he imagined new motives for their actions. During this period of his life, while he was caught in the stress of his creation, Wagner's health suffered but he never wavered, and by December 1852 he was able to write at the end of his huge manuscript: 'Close of the stage-festival play'. By now he had come to see that no known stage could present his vast work adequately: a specially built festival theatre would be required.

So, by 1853 Wagner was at last ready to begin composing the music. For this he began at the beginning with *Das Rheingold*, now reduced from three acts to one. That work took him, amazingly enough, if you consider its complexity and original nature, only some six months. *Die Walküre* was begun in the summer of 1854 and completed in the spring of 1856, when *Siegfried* was started. The first two acts took him from September that year until July 1857. Then came the big break during which he wrote *Tristan und Isolde* and *Die Meistersinger* no less, before he resumed work on *Siegfried* in March 1869. *Götterdämmerung* was begun in the autumn of that year and completed on 21 November 1874.

When Wagner published the libretto of *The Ring* shortly after he had begun work on *Die Meistersinger*, he said that he was blatantly seeking some kind of royal patronage in order to bring *The Ring* to fruition. His prayers were answered in the shape of Ludwig of Bavaria, who became his protector and saw to it that *Das Rheingold* reached the Munich stage in 1869, in a production which did not have the composer's approval, although the public liked it well enough. In spite of his opposition, Wagner could write, a month after the première: 'Even a ridiculous or at any rate unatmospheric and lacklustre performance of the most difficult part of the cycle, *Das Rheingold*, still could not kill the work. On the contrary, it confirmed the opera's power and effectiveness, so that many other opera houses are already considering its production'.

Wagner's dissatisfaction with *Das Rheingold* at Munich did not deter King Ludwig from going ahead with the *Walküre* première. Wagner was conspicuous by his absence from rehearsals and from the first night, which he nevertheless condemned. It took place on 26 June 1870. Wagner's fears about the damage the inadequate staging might do to the future of the work, or even to its reception at the time by the many famous people who attended, were ill-founded. However, he made sure that the last two works of the tetralogy were reserved for Bayreuth, the idea for which was now turning into a reality. At first, Wagner had hoped that the theatre would be in Munich, but the growing hostility to him in the Bavarian capital turned him away from that plan. In 1871 he persuaded the authorities in Bayreuth to provide the land on which to build his theatre and home, and the foundation stone of the opera house was laid on 22 May 1872, when the composer conducted a performance of Beethoven's ninth symphony in the town. The theatre was completed in time for the première of the complete *Ring* cycle in August 1876, conducted by Hans Richter. So the culmination of Wagner's efforts, vaguely discerned thirty years earlier, was at last achieved.

What does it all mean? In spite of the many interpretations and glosses put on it by successive commentators, certain basic ideas were undoubtedly in its creator's mind. *The Ring* is the ultimate example in music of the dictum that all power corrupts, absolute power corrupts absolutely. Those who possess the Ring are corrupted absolutely and are doomed to fall. But the work is possibly something of even greater significance, what Wagner himself, in his essay, *Opera and Drama*, called 'an understandable image of the whole history of mankind from the beginnings of society to the requisite collapse of the state'. Wotan's noble attempt to impose an everlasting order on the world, to give it a moral purpose, comes to nothing through his fatal, although well-meant, act of double-dealing. Even his attempt to redeem his wrongdoing through the independent agency of Siegfried, a seemingly free man who could expiate the guilt of the gods, is doomed to failure because even he is not entirely independent of their sin: his good is tainted by evil. Brünnhilde, unprompted by Wotan, eventually achieves the expiation. Having lost her divinity, having been loved and betrayed by Siegfried, she perceives the need to cleanse the world through the destruction of the tainted gods and restore the symbol of power, the Ring, to the Rhine. And her love is the ennobling factor that makes this something more than a mere deed of destruction.

As Wagner himself wrote: 'A human being is both Man and Woman, and it is only when these two are united that the real human being exists, and thus it is only by love that man and woman reach the full range of humanity. . . .' Hope and love course through the final bars of the vast work. The fable signifies an end and a beginning, and we should not come through its telling and retelling (that is, at first and subsequent encounters) without some sense of enlightenment. Each generation will, of course, relate *The Ring* to its own experience of philosophy, politics, and religion, and thus, like all great works of art, its interpretation and reinterpretation will be unending.

In order for the newcomer to make up his own mind about its meaning, it is essential that he should understand not only its musical structure, although that, in a sense, is a lifetime's work in itself, but also how the musical ideas relate to the text. Wagner was intent, above all, upon propagating dramatic ideas through his music. However much we may be entranced by and absorbed in the astounding musical score, we must correlate it closely to what is being said and done on stage. To do that we must understand what the characters represent, how they are depicted in the work, and how they and their music develop. Let us start with them.

DRAMATIS PERSONAE

The Gods

The noblest race in *The Ring*. Described by Wotan, their ruler, in *Siegfried* as light-spirits who inhabit the cloudy heights. The other gods and goddesses are:

Donner, the god of Thunder (appears in person only in *Das Rheingold*)

Froh, the god of Light and Joy

Loge, god of Fire

Fricka, Wotan's wife, goddess of Marriage

Freia, goddess of Youth and Love

Erda, primeval Earth goddess

The Giants

Simple, strong men, lacking in guile.
Fafner
Fasolt

The Nibelungs

Dwarfs living in caverns below ground, who are full of envy,
    cunning and ambition, and bitterly hostile to the gods.
Alberich
Mime, Alberich's brother
Hagen, Alberich's son by a human, Grimhilde

The Rhinemaidens

A joyous, guileless trio who wish to annul the power of evil.
Woglinde
Wellgunde
Flosshilde

The Valkyries

Warlike yet compassionate, Wotan's daughters mothered by
    Erda (although it has been suggested that only Brünnhilde
    is her child).
Brünnhilde
Waltraute
Gerhilde
Ortlinde
Schwertleite
Helmwige
Siegrune
Grimgerde
Rossweisse

Mortals

Heroes and lesser men and women.
Siegmund and *Sieglinde*, twin children of Wotan by a
    Wälsung
Siegfried, son of Siegmund and Sieglinde

Hunding, Sieglinde's husband
Gutrune and *Gunther*, Gibichungs

Relationships

Wotan's wives: Fricka, his lawful wife; Erda; a mortal
   Wälsung
Wotan's children: Brünnhilde, by Erda; the other Valkyries;
   Siegmund and Sieglinde, the Wälsung twins (by a mortal)
Erda's children: Brünnhilde; The Three Norns
Sieglinde: Hunding, her lawful husband; Siegmund, her twin
   brother and lover
Sieglinde and *Siegmund*: Siegfried, their son
Siegfried, m. Brünnhilde; m. Gutrune
Brünnhilde, m. Siegfried; m. Gunther
Alberich and *Mime*, brothers
Fafner and *Fasolt*, brothers
Gunther and *Gutrune*, brother and sister, children of
   Grimhilde (who does not appear), queen of the Gibichungs
Hagen, half-brother of Gunther and Gutrune, illegitimate
   offspring of Grimhilde by Alberich

Geography

Valhalla, the castle built by the giants on the mountain tops
   for the gods, where the gods dwell.
On the earth's surface
   Riesenheim, home of the giants
   Hunding's hut
   A primeval forest
   Brünnhilde's rock
   The Gibichung castle
   The banks of the Rhine
The waters of the Rhine, where the Rhinemaidens are at
   home
Nibelheim, under the earth, inhabited by the Nibelungs

The Elements and what they signify

Light and Youth: Freia and Froh

Darkness: The Nibelungs
Fire: Loge
Water: The Rhinemaidens
Air (Storm): Donner and the Valkyries
Gold: The Ring and the Nibelung's treasure
Steel: The Sword (Notung)

Symbols and Magic

Ring: Power, endows owner with supernatural strength
Sword: Strength, owes its magic power to Wotan
Spear: Wotan's authority and power
Tarnhelm (Magic Cap): Deceit
Rope of the Norns: Thread of destiny
Golden apples: Grown by Freia, give the gods their eternal
    youth
Draught: Effaces all past memories
Dragon's blood: Enables Siegfried to understand the
    language of the birds

Development of the Characters

Wotan: Although he is the chief of the gods, his power is not
absolute, nor is he the perfect being. As a young man he was
mainly interested in love. That has now been replaced by
ambition, and as *The Ring* begins he is seeking with every
means possible to extend his power by subjecting others to
his will. He embodies the temptation in all to become tyran-
nical, while realizing the danger of such all-embracing power.
He becomes oppressed by the fear of losing his ill-gotten
gains. By listening to the warning of Erda, he escapes at the
eleventh hour from his folly and from the danger of possessing the Ring.

In his fear of being annihilated he resorts to other means to
achieve his will: he sets aside customary morality and tries to
escape from natural laws through Siegmund and Sieglinde.
But, outmanoeuvred by his wife Fricka, he is forced to submit
to the inevitable, abandon his plans, and renounce his ambitions. Heartbroken and weary, he resigns himself to his fate,

and becomes merely a passive spectator of events. Just once more he tries to influence them, to stop Siegfried from fulfilling his destiny, but the last vestige of his power is destroyed and he calmly awaits the approach of his doom, the extinction of his glory.

Fricka: The representative of orthodox morality. Her fundamentally conservative cast of mind cannot grasp the radical intentions of her husband. If the creation of a new race flies in the face of the conventional bonds of marriage, it is not for her. Stern and inexorable, she forces Wotan to abandon his new ideas and to uphold the cause of right as she, with her narrow outlook, views it. Righteous indignation is the victor.

Loge: The Fire god is the representative of intrigue and irresponsibility. His nature is roving and restless, and he possesses a ready and sarcastic wit. He stands apart from, and criticizes, the actions of the gods. His cunning is indispensable to the higher powers he serves, and his cleverness gets others out of tricky situations. In particular, his crafty advice is made use of by Wotan; but in doing so Loge abets his own ends. He has often been described as the cycle's sole intellectual.

Freia: The goddess of Youthful Love. Her gift of the golden apples is essential to the gods' immortality. She is temporarily sacrificed to Wotan's and Fricka's lust for money and power.

Froh: The god of Joy, most anxious to retain Freia, his twin sister. He is a more poetic and sensitive figure than his brother Donner.

Donner: The god of Thunder, and as such a blustering figure, perhaps the aggressive extension of Wotan. He is always intent on achieving things unthinkingly, by violence. At the same time, he can exercise his power positively as when he helps the gods enter Valhalla.

Erda: The primeval earth-mother, who knows all the secrets of nature and destiny. Wagner described her as 'the eternal woman possessed of all the world's wisdom'. She appears in *The Ring* only at moments of uncertainty in order to resolve them, but she gives her advice, imparts her instinctive wisdom, in riddles. At Wotan's bidding, she returns to her eternal sleep.

The Wälsung Twins — Siegmund and Sieglinde: By virtue of their divine origin as Wotan's children, they have a different nature from other mortals. That causes them to be misunderstood and persecuted. Siegmund, in particular, becomes an 'outsider'. Separated as children, each has become isolated. Once brought together again, a mutual sympathy is inevitable. In consummating their incestuous love they break the laws of human morality and are condemned as outcasts. Their separation and death is bound to follow, yet not before they have shown the intensity of love's power.

Brünnhilde: The representative of elevated, as distinct from carnal, love, humanity at its closest to the divine. From her father (Wotan) she has inherited courage and strength, from her mother (Erda) wisdom and foresight. She becomes an active expression of Wotan's will, but a split in that will causes the first conflict in her being. Compassion for the sorrow of Siegmund and Sieglinde resolves the conflict. She thereby frees herself from the gods and escapes their forthcoming annihilation. Having lost the protection of the gods, she has to submit to mortal love. After hesitation she capitulates to human passion, as personified in Siegfried. But in the union she foresees their death and destruction because they will fall victim to evil forces. Only after long anguish and despair does she become enlightened as to their cause. The love in her heart triumphs over care and sorrow, and becomes a divine compassion for suffering humanity. By her self-sacrifice, she redeems the world.

Waltraute: The Valkyrie closest to Brünnhilde, and as such, in *Götterdämmerung* attempts to save the gods from destruction by appealing to Brünnhilde to come to her senses and perceive the danger. But she fails because her reasoning is in vain against the power of love.

The Rhinemaidens: The original guardians of the gold. They also represent the unattainable, untainted image of female beauty as characterized by the mermaid. All unbeknown, they give away to Alberich, the personification of evil, the secret of their gold, and pay the consequences when it is rudely stolen from them. Brünnhilde, having expiated the crimes committed in its name, eventually returns it to them, and they drown Hagen, who would steal the gold and, thereby, start the process all over again.

Alberich: Wotan's antipole, who acquires unlimited power through stealing the gold. He personifies evil because, in a sense, he is the dark side of Wotan; he represents, in fact, the dark, shadowy side in all of us, and the ugly side of passion. He also has a formidable and resolute kind of courage and inner energy. He is willing to sacrifice sensual pleasure for what is, for him, the more compelling call of power that will enable him to tyrannize the world. He scoffs at goodness and nobility, and wishes either to accumulate wealth or to destroy it. When he loses the power of the gold through Loge's deceit, he seeks any and every opportunity to regain it. Only Brünnhilde's divine love finally sets his ambitions at naught.

Mime: Another member of the shadow world, avaricious and treacherous. He is also weak and cowardly, and so falls under the baleful control of Alberich. When Alberich loses his power, Mime becomes a free agent. For his own purposes he is benevolent to Siegfried, keeping the boy ignorant of his origin. His underhand behaviour and attempts at deception bring him deservedly to his death.

Hagen: The personification of hate, he has been brought up by his father, Alberich, to seek revenge. From Alberich he has inherited a hatred of all that is good. He tends to be gloomy, morose and cold; all his energy is spent on regaining the Ring for which purpose he insinuates himself into the confidence of others, making their desires serve his own ends and sacrificing their happiness in his cause. In contrast to his half-brother and half-sister, he is a harsh, sinister figure, a dark shadow in the Gibichung Hall. In the end, he is unable to frustrate the power of love, and meets a well-deserved death.

Gunther: A moral weakling, a man who gets on well enough in life provided too much pressure is not put on him, in which case he is likely to prove inadequate. He is anxious to improve his worldly position, and to do so enlists the aid of his stronger, but more evil half-brother. To satisfy his own desires, he condones wrong-doing, and through that brings about his own downfall and death.

Gutrune: The representative of feminine frailty she is, above all, vulnerable. Like her brother Gunther she is capable of coping with normal human situations but not with the tremendous events with which she becomes involved. Although she wittingly sacrifices another woman's happiness to her own desires, and is even jealous of Brünnhilde, she enjoys her brief period of happiness by forgetting her guilt. Only when the consequences of her evil-doing become clear to her does she have any remorse and realize the effects of her own action. Eventually her weak personality is subsumed in the grandeur of her rival's.

Fasolt: The more gentle of the giants, less avaricious than Fafner, more susceptible to the charms of Freia, and reluctant to sacrifice her for the sake of the gold, and therefore for power. He becomes the first victim of the Ring's curse.

Siegfried: The image of a hero, a true child of nature, without malice, above fear, coursing with untold vitality. He might be

an unsympathetic hero were it not for his moments of introspection. At first he is all youthful impetuosity, unaware of
his destiny. Having forged the sword, he clears all obstacles
in his path by his undaunted fearlessness and becomes master
of the gold, and so of untold wealth. He wins the love of the
noblest woman in the world (Brünnhilde). However, through
the agency of a draught that makes him forget the past, he
becomes the unwitting accomplice in a plot that will destroy
him.

THE SYMBOLS

The Gold: In its natural state, it is guarded in the Rhine by
the Rhinemaidens, and remains harmless. Once transferred
from its natural element, its form and properties are changed.
In the hands of an evil person such as Alberich, it becomes a
powerful force, conferring (in the shape of the Ring) omnipotence on its possessor, enabling him to obtain all he desires.
Once Alberich has it, he stores it in order to further his plans
for worldly domination. When Wotan seizes it from the
dwarf, it becomes part of the ransom to free Freia from the
giants, who immediately fight over it. Fasolt is killed. Fafner,
with the help of the Tarnhelm, takes the shape of a dragon
and keeps guard over what has become his hoard. Having
killed him, Siegfried does not realize the value of the gold,
taking only the Ring and Tarnhelm, the magic cap.

The Ring: The more specific symbol of omnipotence, endow-
ing its possessor with supernatural strength, with superhuman power over his fellows. Alberich has had it created from
the gold, which he has gained through his renunciation of
love, and through its power he hopes to destroy all that is
good in the world. When it is wrenched from him by Wotan,
he curses it, so that it becomes the cause of eternal misery in
the world. Indeed, its very existence causes the end of existence. It forms the object of plots and intrigues on earth. All
wish to possess it, but those who do fall victim to Alberich's
curse, which passes from it only when Brünnhilde, after the

trial and anxieties it has brought upon her, restores it to its native element.

The Tarnhelm: The cap is the symbol of deception, enabling its owner to become invisible. Mime, unknowingly, has made this powerful weapon for his master Alberich, and it becomes a factor for evil. However, Alberich is hoist with his own petard when the cunning Loge traps him with the aid of the Tarnhelm. Fafner, as we have noted, uses it to turn himself into a dragon; Siegfried learns of its power only from Hagen and through it deceives Brünnhilde.

The Sword: This is the symbol of strength and the burning force of life. Siegmund comes to possess it through the love of Sieglinde, but Wotan, who has presented Siegmund with this life force, nullifies its power when he is forced to shatter it by Fricka's insistence on the upholding of marital law. Its fragments are inherited by Siegmund's son, Siegfried, through Mime, who is powerless to recreate this life force. Only Siegfried is able to refashion the sword, and use it as a weapon. It is now seemingly invested with superhuman power as it strikes down evil, breaks the spear, and cuts through Brünnhilde's armour, losing its power only when Siegfried betrays Brünnhilde.

The Spear: This is the symbol of Wotan's authority while that lasts. Through it he has subjected others to his will, and by it he prevents strife between gods and giants. It is his ego, and its power is eventually broken by the superior power of the Sword, representing youthful strength and love.

Valhalla: This castle of the gods is the symbol of power, whose price is the loss of love and youth. Paid for by the gold, it comes under that symbol's evil curse. It also represents the old order that is passing away. Eventually, without the presence of Brünnhilde, its noblest inhabitant, it becomes a loveless, careworn place where Wotan awaits his doom. Its false glory is eventually destroyed, and with it the existing order of things, through Brünnhilde's new power of love.

Das Rheingold

The introduction to the tetralogy begins with the famous, long, E flat chord deep down in the double-basses, representing primeval purity before it is smirched by any evil thought. Gradually the sounds rise and swell, become more intense, until the music shapes itself into the first definite motif, that of the Rhine itself, on the flutes and bassoons, a motif that, like most of the others in the whole work, in not static but fluid in concept, both changing its original meaning and developing from it. As long as that is understood, no harm can come from identifying a motif when it first appears (1).*

Scene 1

When the waters seem to reach full tide, the curtain rises. The scene is the bottom of the Rhine. In a greenish twilight, lighter at the top, darker below, whirling waters and rugged rocks are visible. Near the bottom, the water becomes something of a damp mist, so that a space as high as a man from the ground seems to be quite free of the water that flows, as if in cloud formation, over the dark river bed. The rock faces rise everywhere from the deep and mark the sides of the stage. The entire bed of the river is made up of jagged rocks, and so is nowhere flat: deep gorges are to be imagined everywhere.

* Figures in brackets refer to music examples, to be found in Appendix 1.

Round one rock in the centre of the stage, towering above the rest into the brighter part, one of the Rhinemaidens, Woglinde, swims with graceful strokes. (These are Wagner's own stage directions, all of which will be included throughout.)

Woglinde's clear song rises above the orchestra, like the first ray of light piercing the darkness. Wellgunde, her sister, joins her in a game of chase while Flosshilde, the third maiden, chides them for neglecting to guard the gold. 'Weia! Wage! Woge!', they sing, their song representing the voice of Nature; it resembles, too, the sound of the waves (2). While they have been laughing and playing, the Nibelung Alberich comes into view, a sinister shadow on the happy scene, musically represented by the introduction of darker elements into the score. From his home under the waters, he comes to watch the Rhinemaidens, filled with sensual desires. He calls to them and then tries to join in their game, so as to catch one of them. The grotesque spectacle of the repulsive dwarf makes them laugh with scorn. They entice him, by approaching him, and then, when he tries to grasp one of them, quickly escaping, repelled by his ugliness. Flosshilde alone pretends to take pity on him, and in an encouraging manner sings beguilingly to him. He responds in like manner. For a moment she has him in her arms, then breaks cruelly away. Frantic and frustrated he swears he will have one or other of them; he clambers clumsily and menacingly over the rocks (this is amply illustrated in the music), while the Rhinemaidens continue to mock him, as they elude his grasp.

Suddenly, in the midst of his impotent rage, Alberich's attention is diverted from the Rhinemaidens to a magical golden light, which sinks down through the water, while shining rays come from the high rock in the centre of the stream. Through a gentle shimmer on the strings gleams the motif of the gold (3) which will recur throughout the whole work. The Rhinemaidens hail with delight the gold they harbour. Their cry of joy forms the second half of the gold motif (4) betokening its beauty and purity, a source at this stage only of innocent pleasure to the maidens who guard it. They invite Alberich to revel with them in the golden glory. By their heedless chatter, they now reveal to the Nibelung the secret power of the gold: that he who could fashion a ring from the gold would master the world; here, on the oboes, the motif of the Ring descends and rises in thirds (5). Flosshilde thinks that they have said too much already, but Wellgunde and Woglinde remind her what protects the gold: only he who forswears the delights of love could transform the gold into a ring to the motif of renunciation (6), and Alberich, of all creatures, is least likely to follow that path. They do not understand their gnome, for to the accompaniment of the first gold motif and the motif of renunciation, he says to himself that he intends to threaten the treasure. By a frantic effort, he manages to clamber up the centre rock and with a cry of renunciation abjures love as he seizes the gold, while the frightened Rhinemaidens flee from him. Alberich then rapidly descends into the deep as the first gold motif (3) dies away in a sorrowful minor key, ending in the motif of renunciation (6).

Now *The Ring*'s first transformation takes place as the waves gradually disappear, giving place first to clouds and then to mist, which in turn is displaced by a mountain top.

Scene 2

An open space on a mountain top. Daybreak with growing brightness illuminates a castle with gleaming battlements. Between that and the foreground, where Wotan and Fricka are asleep, we are to imagine the flowing Rhine. The castle becomes completely visible. Fricka awakens; she catches sight of it. From the trombones and tubas rises the noble Valhalla motif (7). Valhalla is the castle in which the gods are to dwell from now on, and from where Wotan, their head, intends to increase his authority. On awakening, Fricka, when she sees the castle, calls Wotan to awake from his vision of power and glory – what she considers to be his deceptive dream. Wotan rises, power-drunk, greets the castle as the realization of what he has willed. Fricka reminds him that a price has to be paid to the giants, who have built the castle for him and that the promised reward is Freia, the fair goddess of beauty and youth, who guards the rejuvenating apples. At this we hear for the first time, on cellos and basses, the motif of Wotan's spear, which seems graphically to describe the bringing down of the spear's point to the ground, a symbol of Wotan's supposed authority (8). It is also a symbol of his treaty with the giants, a treaty he has been advised to enter into by Loge, the cunning god of Fire. Fricka reproaches him for so lightly bartering away Freia but Wotan retorts that he had never seriously intended fulfilling his side of the bargain, and is depending on Loge to come to some arrangement with the giants.

Freia herself now enters in great distress, to a descending motif on the violins that will be associated with her throughout the work (9). She runs in terror towards Fricka and Wotan, seeking their protection from the giants. Wotan, remaining complacent, is certain Loge will cheat them out of Freia. As Freia appeals to her brothers Donner and Froh for help, the giants themselves can be heard approaching. Their rough character and clumsy tread is well expressed by their motif (10). Fasolt, the softer of the two giants, who is infatuated with Freia, patiently puts his case to Wotan. He and his brother have laboured mightily to fulfil the god's wish for his fortress. Now Wotan must pay the agreed reward: the beautiful Freia is forfeit to them. Fafner, the more crafty and uncouth of the two, points out to Fasolt that they need Freia in order to deprive the gods of her life-enhancing gifts, without which they will weaken and die. They are just about to carry out their intention to drag her away when Froh and Donner enter, the latter raising his hammer to strike down the giants. Wotan interposes his spear between the combatants; and at this apposite moment Loge enters much to Wotan's relief as he has begun to be worried about the uncomfortable situation. Loge is accompanied by various fragments of motifs, each suggestive of his crafty, elusive nature, his slippery cunning and restlessness, no more controllable than the fire that is his element. Wotan reproaches him for not arriving sooner, and asks him for a way out of the situation. Loge resents Wotan's attitude and gives an evasive answer. Pressed harder by Wotan, he asks how he shall find that which does not exist. Loge's ironical, treacherous attitude angers the forthright Froh and Donner, who are again inclined to use force. Again Wotan intervenes. Fasolt and Fafner are more insistent in their demands for payment. Wotan demands from Loge a more logical reply.

Loge launches into what is known as his Narration, a lyrical episode in a fundamentally dramatic and expository texture. He states equivocally that his lot is always a thankless one. To the accompaniment of Freia's sweet music, he tells how he has scoured the world for a substitute payment, but wherever he went on earth, in air and water, no living thing would renounce love, until he came upon Alberich, who had cast it aside at the sight of the gold, which he had robbed from the Rhinemaidens. They had implored Loge to carry their tale of woe to Wotan, and beg him to punish the thief. (Throughout the Narration, Wagner begins to deploy his motifs with the kind of freedom and insight that will grow in authority as *The Ring* proceeds.) Loge ends his tale by saying complacently that he has now fulfilled his promise to the Rhinemaidens. This angers Wotan. How can he help others when he himself is so deep in the mire?

The giants also have been listening carefully, and are now struck by the power of the Ring. Fricka, for her part, thinks it would make a beautiful ornament, and Loge further ensnares her by suggesting that its possession would ensure her husband's fidelity. Wotan, whose mind remains fixed on winning absolute power, inquires of Loge how it would be possible to gain the Ring. Wotan cannot bring himself to forswear love and, even if he did, it is too late: Alberich has already done so and is in consequence in possession of the Ring. How else may the Ring be got? By theft, Loge suddenly suggests. The Nibelung had stolen it from the Rhinemaidens, so why not steal it from him, as long as it is given back to them. To the giants, the possession of the gold seems more desirable than the possession of Freia; they, like Alberich, are willing to renounce love, in the person of the goddess, if Wotan will get the gold for them. Having announced their wish, they carry off Freia as a hostage for the gold, in spite of Wotan's remonstrations.

In a marvellously descriptive passage, Loge recounts how the giants depart, roughly carrying Freia over the rocks through the valley across the Rhine. He then perceives that the gods, without Freia's life-giving apples, are turning pale and impotent, while a grey mist sinks over the scene. With sudden determination, Wotan resolves to take the gold from Alberich so as to restore the gods' eternal youth. He disappears with Loge into a crevice in the rocks, to descend to Nibelheim, the underground home of the dwarfs who work as smiths. The long passage accompanying the change of scene depicts the journey of the two gods, employs motifs already heard, and introduces the graphic Nibelung motif, the metallic sound of which resembles the regular fall of a hammer on an anvil (11).

Scene 3

The third scene represents Nibelheim, a form of subterranean vault, surrounded by rock. The light diffused over the scene is subdued and reddish. Alberich emerges from one of the cave's openings, dragging by the ear Mime, his brother dwarf, who is shrieking. Mime, most skilful of the smiths, has been trying a little sharp practice, possibly trying to catch Alberich in some trap. To guard against that, Alberich has forced Mime to make a magic cap, the Tarnhelm, which will enable him to be everywhere at all times among his worker-slaves. By putting it on, its owner can make himself invisible, or change into any form he wishes. The motif of the Tarn-helm (12) with its strange chords rising and falling on the horns, expresses the dark, dangerous power of the cap. Mime has put all his subtle skill into making it, according to Alberich's instructions. Although Mime suspects that the cap has hidden power, he has not been able to find out what that power is. He is not left long in ignorance. Alberich no sooner has it in his hands than he tests its power by making himself invisible to the astonished dwarf, whom he unmercifully beats and pinches, and then leaves howling on the ground. Alberich exalts in his power and disappears. Mime is still moaning in the corner where Alberich has left him, when Wotan and Loge enter. They learn from him the cause of his misery: the poor working conditions in Nibelheim and Alberich's unmerciful rule over his own brother and over the whole Nibelung race. Mime only wishes that he had realized what the spell of the Tarnhelm was so that he could have used it against his enslaver. His narrative is couched in the whining, small-scale accents so expressive of his grotesque body and mean spirit.

Alberich now reappears, driving before him a crowd of frightened Nibelungs, laden with gold, which they pile up into a heap, amid scolding and blows from their master. To the motif of the Ring (5), followed by that of his triumph, sometimes known as the servitude motif (13), Alberich draws the Ring from his finger and drives the Nibelungs, screaming, from the scene. Suddenly he catches sight of Wotan and Loge, and asks them curtly what they are doing in his domain. Wotan explains that rumours of Alberich's fame have reached them, and they have come out of curiosity. Alberich believes that it is jealousy that has brought them. Loge interposes, and asks Alberich if he does not remember his friend, but Alberich answers that Loge is now a friend of the gods, and he therefore no longer trusts his friendship. Alberich remains lordly and defiant. He shows the two gods the treasure, explaining that what they see there is but a miserable little heap compared with the dimensions it will soon attain, and that with this treasure he is going to make himself master of the whole world. The motif of the treasure (14) wells up from the depths of the orchestra on bassoon and bass clarinet, and ascends the scale in sinister, threatening tones. The gods, who live, laugh and love on the heights, are the object of Alberich's bitterest hatred: they, too, shall come under his dominion. He declares that all living beings shall renounce love, as he has done; like him, all shall be greedy for gold, and shall be its slaves. A demoniacal rage against all that is pure and noble possesses this son of darkness, and his warning to Wotan to beware is full of menace and scorn. For this incarnation of evil, envy and hatred, Wagner creates a response as powerful as anything previously heard in music, an outburst of rage, terrifying in its power.

Not unnaturally, it arouses Wotan's own anger, but Loge speedily intervenes and advises the chief of the gods to control his wrath. Then he turns to Alberich and proceeds to outwit the boastful dwarf with his cunning. Everyone, of course, must wonder at Alberich's power, Loge says, but supposing someone among the Nibelungs tried to wrest it from him? What protection has he? Alberich prides himself on having foreseen that possibility, and has made Mime fashion the Tarnhelm, now hanging at his side, with which he can transform himself into whatever shape he wishes. Loge persuades him to show off its magic properties. Alberich puts on the cap and changes into a huge dragon, graphically portrayed in the orchestra's brass by its motif (15). Loge pretends to quail in terror. Wotan laughs. But, Loge asks, can Alberich also turn himself into something correspondingly small? If you wish, says the vainglorious dwarf, and becomes a toad. At a sudden command from Loge, Wotan puts his foot on the little creature, and so the two capture Alberich, who is instantly returned to his own form. Loge binds him, and they drag him screaming up to the earth's surface to a triumphant combination of various motifs, including a prominent appearance of the Ring theme (5).

The scene changes but in the opposite direction. Again the smithy is passed, with a repetition of the Nibelung hammering (11), and there is continual upward motion in the music. Bringing Alberich, fettered, with them, Wotan and Loge climb up out of the crevice. Meanwhile, Wagner's tone painting continues on the orchestra.

Scene 4

Once more an open plateau on the mountain top. Mist still hangs over it, as at the end of Scene 2. Wotan and Loge set down their prisoner on a rock, and Loge dances round him, teasing him. Alberich threatens him with vengeance, but Loge comments ironically that in order to carry them out he must first free himself. As the price of his freedom, Wotan demands the Nibelung gold. Alberich uses the Ring to call the Nibelungs to rise from their subterranean homes and bring the treasure. The Ring (5) and servitude motifs (13) sound softly in the orcherstra, gradually growing louder as the Nibelungs approach. They crowd on to the scene and pile up the hoard on stage. Alberich bemoans the fact that his minions should see him thus enslaved and, once their work is done, kisses the Ring and stretches it out imperiously. As if struck by a blow, the Nibelungs rush in terror into the crevice whence they came, and quickly pass down it. This terrifying episode, one of Wagner's most wonderful creations, is accompanied by the motif of servitude (13), thundered out by the trumpets and trombones.

Once the turmoil has died away, Alberich demands to be set free, and to be allowed to take the Tarnhelm with him. Wotan contemptuously rejects the request. Alberich curses him, but then reflects that Mime can easily make another cap. Wotan now declares that he also covets the Ring on Alberich's finger. Alberich pleads that he would rather lose his life than give up the Ring. He reminds Wotan of the unholy means by which he, Alberich, came into possession of it. The Nibelung, however, sinned only against himself: Wotan, in possessing the Ring, would sin against all that was and is to be. As Ernest Newman* has pointed out: 'Wagner, it will be seen, is holding the moral scales fairly between the two. For the first time, the central, ethical problem of the great drama comes clearly into sight.'

Alberich's words are in vain. Wotan himself (significantly,

* *Wagner Nights*, Putnam & Co., 1968 (hardback edn); Pan Books, 1977 (paperback Picador edn).

not Loge) takes the Ring from him by force; and with a cry Alberich sinks into an attitude of abject misery. Wotan puts the Ring on his finger and, contemplating it, muses that it will make him lord of the world. Then, in a forceful monologue, Alberich, now set free, declares that in order that the results of his own crime may continue and bring similar misery and final annihilation to the gods, he will curse the ring – death to whomever may wear it. No happiness shall be attached to its possession, its owner shall suffer torments of anxiety, and those who do not have it shall be consumed with envy. It shall bring misery and death to all alike until it comes again into Alberich's hands. This curse, in his hour of distress, he places on the Ring. Two motifs dominate this outburst, that of annihilation, sometimes known as Alberich's revenge motif (16), and the curse motif (17). With these fearful words, Alberich disappears through a crevice in the rock. After his furious departure, amply depicted in the orchestra, a deceptive calm returns to the scene as Wotan is lost in dreams, contemplating the Ring. The mists disperse as the gods return, asking Wotan how he has fared. He points to the hoard and declares that it is Freia's ransom. The motif of annihilation in the orchestra (16) denies the force of what he is saying and tells us of his self-delusion. To their motif (10), the giants return, dragging Freia with them. The gods regain their vitality, but mist still hovers over Valhalla. Fricka embraces her sister.

Fasolt, the gentler-natured of the giants, gives up Freia reluctantly, and wishes for the gold to be piled so high that Freia will be hidden from his sight. The two giants place Freia in the middle. Then they thrust their clubs in the ground on each side of her so as to measure her exact height and breadth. Loge and Froh quickly assemble the treasure between the clubs. Fafner, with rough gestures, presses the heap tightly together, then bends down looking for holes, and says he can still see Freia through a chink. While the gods can hardly contain themselves for their rage, Fafner demands more and more. Freia's hair still shines through, so the Tarnhelm is demanded. Fasolt, still grieving in the most tender way over Freia's loss (Wagner, like all great opera composers, has the ability to take the part of whichever character he happens at that moment to be portraying) discovers a further gap. To stop up that, Fafner points to the Ring on Wotan's finger. Wotan says peremptorily that he will not part with it.

Loge comments rather wryly that the Ring is actually the property of the Rhinemaidens. As Wotan will not relent, even when Loge reminds him of his (Loge's) promise to them, Fasolt angrily pulls Freia from behind the pile and is about to carry her off screaming when Donner demands that Wotan give up the Ring. They all stand perplexed. As Wotan turns angrily away, the stage suddenly darkens and a blue light breaks from a cleft in the rocks. Erda appears and rises from below. Her noble face is framed by black hair.

Accompanied by motifs 1 and 2, now melded and in the minor to suggest her primeval character, Erda declares that she is gifted with knowledge of the secret forces of nature, forces that direct and govern all that is, before which even gods must give way. She warns Wotan that the gods' day is coming to an end, and a new motif appears, depicting the coming twilight of the gods (18). This is what has brought her from the bowels of the earth. She advises Wotan to avoid the curse attached to the Ring. She sinks slowly as the blue light begins to fade. Then, after a further warning, she disappears entirely. Wotan tries to follow her, but Froh and Fricka effectively prevent him. Her warning has not, however, been in vain. The gods watch Wotan anxiously. After meditating for a little, he rouses himself, seizes his spear and brandishes it as the sign of a bold decision (8). He gives up the Ring to the giants, throwing it on the pile. They release Freia, who hurries happily over to the gods, and they delightedly embrace her. Fafner at once spreads out a huge sack in which he begins to pack the treasure. Fasolt immediately begins to quarrel with him over the division of the spoils. He is reminded by Fafner that he was more keen on having the girl. The sordid wrangle continues, particularly over possession of

the Ring, until the curse claims its first victim: Fasolt is felled
by a single blow from his fellow giant. Fafner quickly seizes
the Ring from the dying Fasolt. He puts it in his sack, and
loads up the rest of the treasure. The gods, appalled, look on
in solemn silence.

Wotan for the first time realizes the terrible power of the
curse, and its motif (17) pounds out in the orchestra. Loge
points out how lucky Wotan has been to have it thus taken
from him, but Wotan is concerned only to seek out Erda and
to learn from her how to banish the fear and anxiety that
have taken possession of him. Fricka asks him why he does
not now enter the castle. He wryly comments that Valhalla
was paid for in bad money. Pointing to the background still
veiled in mist, Donner decides to clear the air with a
thunderstorm. Donner's invocation to the elements (19) is a
picture in sound from the horns, accompanied by the violins
and cellos, while the basses add touches of thunder. Donner
has mounted a high rock overhanging the valley and swings
his hammer. Eventually he disappears behind a thundercloud
that grows thicker and blacker. His hammer blow, heard
striking hard on the rock, causes a flash of lightning to shoot
from the cloud, followed by a violent clap of thunder. Suddenly the clouds lift, and Donner and Froh are again visible.
From their feet a rainbow spans the Rhine, stretching across
the valley to the castle, now bathed in the evening sunshine.
The rainbow forms a bridge to Valhalla. Wotan and the other
gods are speechless at the wonderful sight. Fafner has meanwhile completed his packing, put the enormous sack on his
back and made off during the thunderstorm.

Wotan greets the castle with glowing words, as Wagner
unleashes a flood of glorious sound. Suddenly, the god is
struck by a great idea. He picks up a sword that had been
part of the treasure and, pointing it towards the castle, solemnly salutes it as the trumpet intones the sword motif (20).
Taking Fricka by the hand he leads her over the bridge. Froh,
Freia and Donner follow. The mocking Loge casts his baleful
eye over the supposedly triumphant scene, declaring that the

gods are hurrying to their end. Although he is apparently reluctant to share in any more of their activities, he is non-chalantly about to join them when he hears the voices of the Rhinemaidens bewailing their lost treasure. Wotan, with one foot on the bridge, turns round and asks what the sound is. When Loge informs him, Wotan tells him to stop the Rhinemaidens from irritating the gods. Loge, with his usual sarcasm, calls down the river that their gold is lost to them and they had better sun themselves in the newly acquired glory of the gods, who now laugh as they begin to cross the bridge. The Rhinemaidens' lament resounds ever more poignantly but it is drowned in the magnificent confidence of the Valhalla motif (6), a grand triumphal march into a home that will not prove as safe as it now seems: the doom foreseen by Loge will come about.

In *Das Rheingold* the main lines of *The Ring*'s dramatic conflict are set out, and so are many of the cycle's main musical ideas. Alberich's lust for power overcomes his instinctive sensuality, and the frustration of his aim of world domination sets in motion the chain of succeeding disasters. His overweening ambition is contrasted with the fundamental innocence of the Rhinemaidens. That innocence is destroyed both by Alberich's schemings and by Wotan's willingness to trade Freia for the outward trappings of power and prestige; that willingness is in turn complicated by Wotan's feelings towards his wife Fricka, personification of his nagging conscience. Then there is the cause of the giants, who seem to have right on their side as they make an unanswerable claim for their treaty with Wotan to be observed. Loge, duplicity personified, is an outsider, able cynically to view the action of Nibelungs and gods, but as Wotan's accomplice also able, with the help of his wily intelligence, to find a solution to his problem.

Over and above the dramatic and psychological fascination of the work's first part is its musical richness and control. Arguably it is the furthest of all Wagner's works from conventional opera. Incontrovertibly, it is the most varied in character, Wagner reflecting his new-won freedom and mastery in effortless depiction of its multifarious characters. The primal innocence and beauty of the Rhinemaidens, the boasting malevolence of Alberich, the galumphing, crude attitudes of the giants, the false sense of power represented by Wotan and Valhalla, the cringing, whimpering fear of Mime, all are unerringly brought before us by Wagner's genius. At the same time, description never interferes with the steady development of the story. The work's other great musical achievement comes in the three transformation scenes, which introduce a new factor into operatic writing. With unfailing mastery, Wagner moves us through his orchestral illustration from the Rhine to Valhalla to Nibelheim and back again to Valhalla. The timbre, the feeling of *Das Rheingold*, as of all four parts of the cycle, is quite individual, tending to be highly dramatic, almost Beethovenian, in its symphonic structure and dynamic pulse, less grand, less leisurely in its development than the later works, more direct in its appeal.

Die Walküre

ACT 1

The prelude to this work forms a striking contrast to the state of primeval peace at the opening of *Das Rheingold*. The second part of the drama opens with the orchestral representation of a distant storm in the forest. The wind sweeps through the violins while the notes on the cellos and basses resemble the footsteps of a man struggling to find his way through the tempest and moving heavily, as if he were growing weary. The music rises and swells as the storm approaches, then dies down again into a murmur as the raging of the elements seems to abate; the flashes of lightning grow less frequent, and the peals of thunder are distant.

Scene 1

When the curtain rises, we see the interior of a hut. In the centre there is the trunk of a huge ash tree whose strong roots stretch all along the ground. The tree is separated from its top by a roof cut so that the trunk and the branches pass through holes made to fit them precisely. We are to imagine that the foliage spreads out above the roof. With the tree trunk as its central point, a room has been built. The walls are made of rough logs covered with woven rugs. In the foreground on the right is the fireplace, whose chimney reaches the roof from the side. Behind the fireplace is an inner room, a kind of store-room, reached by a few wooden steps; in front of it is a plaited rug, half drawn back. Behind is the main door, fitted

with a simple wooden latch. On the left is a door to the
bedroom, also approached by some steps. Further forward,
also on the left side is a table with a big bench on the wall
behind, and wooden stools in front of it.

Siegmund hastily opens the main door and enters. It is
nearly evening; the storm is subsiding. He keeps his hand on
the latch for a moment and looks round the room. He
appears exhausted by some tremendous exertion; his clothes
and his appearance suggest that he a fugitive. Seeing nobody,
he closes the door behind him, walks to the fireplace and
throws himself down on the rug, exhausted. A few low notes
merge on the cellos out of the storm music from Siegmund's
motif, its falling seconds representing pain of soul and body
(21). In his search for shelter Siegmund has arrived unknowingly at the home of his long-lost twin sister, Sieglinde. She
enters from the inner room, assuming that her husband has
returned. Her look changes from gravity to surprise when she
sees a stranger lying by the fireplace. Bending over the half-
conscious Siegmund she tries to see if he is ill or only sleeping,
at which the orchestra plays softly her motif of tenderness
and compassion (22). This is soon subtly and psychologically
blended with Siegmund's motif so that there can be no doubt
of the mingling of their destinies. Suddenly, Siegmund raises
his head and cries for water. As the orchestra expresses all the
sympathy aroused in Sieglinde by Siegmund, she fetches him
spring-water in a drinking-horn. When he has quenched his
thirst, his glance falls on her, and he observes her with growing interest: the motif of their dawning love resounds for the
first time, softly on the cellos (23). In answer to his question,
Sieglinde says that this house and this woman belong to
Hunding, and she bids him await Hunding's return. Siegmund says that her husband will not be troubled by a
wounded man. Sieglinde anxiously asks to see the wounds;
he replies that they are only slight. Sitting up on the rug,
Siegmund pulls himself together and stoutly declares that, in
spite of being wounded, he is still able to resist his enemies,
although his shield and spear were destroyed in his recent

fight. Besides, he has gained new strength from encountering Sieglinde, who now offers him a horn filled with mead from the store-room. He consents to drink from it only after she has first tasted it. Sieglinde sips from the horn and gives it back to Siegmund; as he takes a long drink, he looks at her with growing sympathy. Then he slowly puts down the horn, very much moved, sighs deeply and gazes sadly at the ground. The orchestra softly intones the motifs associated with the pair, showing the growing rapport between the two.

Siegmund, now refreshed and strengthened, rises to his feet and prepares to leave. He tells Sieglinde that he is born to suffer, that he is dogged by misery and misfortune wherever he goes and does not want to bring them upon her. As he moves towards the door, she cries out with abandon that he does not bring misfortune to a house where it already exists. Siegmund is deeply moved, gazing into Sieglinde's face until she lowers her eyes in embarrassment and sadness, while the motif of their doomed love wells up in the orchestra (24). After a long silence, Siegmund turns back, and declares that his name is Wehwalt, woeful, and he will await Hunding. The common suffering of the twins links them; they are drawn to each other by love. The subsequent union of brother and sister, irreconcilable with human morality, assumes a different complexion when judged by the symbolical nature of the whole work, and the mythological sources from which it is derived, such unions being common among the gods and goddesses of legend. Their blood relationship is merely the outward symbol of the affinity of two divine natures that complement each other in the evolution of the perfect hero. As Robert Donington puts it: 'Whatever our ingrained resistance to the idea of incest in the ordinary outside world, we are completely on the side of the lovers as we sit watching them in the opera-house. We share in Wagner's own feeling that the world has blossomed into warmth and fruitfulness after the strained, inhibited congestion of Wotan's plotting and Alberich's hatred in *Rhinegold*.'*

* The Ring and its Symbols. Robert Donington.

Scene 2

Such sympathetic thoughts are rudely interrupted by a harsh, rough although somewhat heroic motif on the horns (25) which announces Hunding's arrival. It partly resembles the motifs of the Nibelung (11) and of the giants (10), for his character has some of their barbaric elements in it. Hunding leads his horse into the stable outside (an action, like so many demanded by Wagner's libretto, seldom if ever seen on-stage). Quickly Sieglinde opens the door for her husband. Hunding, armed with a spear and shield, stops in the door-way as he catches sight of Siegmund, then turns with a stern look to Sieglinde. She explains how she found Siegmund lying exhausted on the hearth, and how she tended him. As he removes his armour and gives it to Sieglinde, Hunding declares that his hearth and house are sacred, and roughly orders her to set out the meal. While she does so, she involuntarily looks again at Siegmund; Hunding, too, watches the stranger and is struck by his likeness to Sieglinde. He hides his suspicions and turns rather nonchalantly to Siegmund who, in reply to Hunding's question, says he had made his way through forest, field, and thicket. Distress and storm chased him. He knows not how he came or whither.

Hunding seats himself at table and motions Siegmund to join him, declaring that this is Hunding's house and that his kinsmen dwell in the surrounding estates. Can he now tell Hunding his name? Siegmund sits down at the table, and looks thoughtfully ahead of him. Sieglinde sits next to Hunding, opposite Siegmund, and fixes an eager, expectant gaze on him. Observing them both, Hunding says that perhaps Siegmund will tell his tale to Hunding's wife. Eagerly Sieglinde puts the question, and gazing into her eyes, Siegmund begins his weird, wild narration.

Siegmund's father was called Wolfe. He himself had a twin-sister. One day Wolfe and his son came home from a hunt in the woods to find their dwelling sacked by enemies, the house burnt down, the mother murdered, and no trace of the sister to be found. The Neidungs, a cruel band of ruffians, had wrought this havoc. Despised and hunted by their enemies, father and son lived for a long time in the wild forest. Turning to Hunding, Siegmund says that a Wölfing, a wolf-cub, tells this tale, to which Hunding replies that he has heard of that warlike pair but never knew Wolfe or Wölfing. Sieglinde urges Siegmund to go on with his story, asking where his father may be now. He says that he had become separated from his father in a fight, and had lost track of him. He had sought him everywhere but found only a wolfskin in the forest. A brief recollection of the Wotan-Valhalla motif (7) hints at who this father may really be.

In his loneliness, Wölfing left the forest to mingle with his fellow-men, but found no friends, meeting only with contempt and anger. Wherever he sought for happiness, he found only sorrow. He therefore named himself Wehwalt, Woeful. As he looks up at Sieglinde, he notices her look of understanding, and the motif of their love (23) is tenderly breathed in the orchestra. Hunding's grim comment is that the Norns who gave him this fate evidently did not love him. Sieglinde says that only cowards fear someone who travels alone and unarmed, then begs the guest to tell them why he is weaponless. Becoming increasingly excited, he relates how a girl was forced by her family into a loveless marriage. He fought for her and killed her brother, but friends and serfs rushed in overpowering numbers upon him. For some time he was able to protect himself and the girl but eventually his spear and shield were hacked to pieces. The girl died; he managed to escape. From all this we gather that Siegmund is the typical 'outsider', a man set apart from others.

As he ends his story, Siegmund looks at Sieglinde and says with pained sadness that she must now know why he is not called Friedmund, Peaceful. The words are intoned, and a thinking tenor can make a profound impression here, to the accompaniment of the motif of the Wälsungs, sombre and tragic (26), its similarity to the Valhalla motif (7) showing the divine origin of the twins. Siegmund now gets up and walks to the fireplace, while Sieglinde, looking pale and shocked, gazes at the ground. Hunding, whose face has grown darker and darker during Siegmund's narration, because he has recognized in Siegmund the man he has recently been called out to fight with, now realizes that he has his enemy on his own hearth. He says that he knows of a savage race who hold nothing sacred that others honour. He was called to take vengeance on this clan but arrived too late. Walking upstage, he declares that he will give Siegmund shelter for a single night: in the morning he will have to defend himself. Sieglinde comes anxiously between the two men, but is roughly ordered by her husband to leave the room, prepare his night draught, and await him in bed.

She remains still and thoughtful for some time, then moves to the store-room where she again stands pensive before opening the cupboard and filling a drinking-horn with spices from a pot. Then she turns towards Siegmund whose eyes have been on her continuously. But Hunding is watching them intently and Sieglinde hurries to the bedroom. On the steps she gives a meaningful look at Siegmund to indicate a place on the trunk of the tree, at which point we hear the sword motif from *Das Rheingold* (20). With a violent gesture, Hunding sends her away. One more glance at Siegmund and she is gone, closing the door behind her, Hunding's harsh motif (25) breaks the silence. After giving Siegmund one last warning, he collects his weapons and follows her.

Scene 3

Siegmund is left alone on the hearth. It is now night; there is only a glimmer from the fire. Siegmund sinks on to the rug in front of it and gazes silently before him. He has much to think about and is obviously agitated. Suddenly he recalls that his father has promised him a sword, which he would find in his greatest distress. He is alone and weaponless in his enemy's house, and he sees here, miserable like himself and in the power of the rough Hunding, a woman beautiful and dignified. He calls desperately and appealingly on Wälse (the name by which he knew his father). At his cry, the logs in the fireplace collapse and the fire comes to life, throwing a red glow on the place on the tree trunk which Sieglinde had indicated, where the hilt of a buried sword is now distinctly visible. Siegmund does not notice it, but thinks only of the brightness in Sieglinde's eyes, like the last rays of the setting sun before it sank behind the hills. Now the fire in the hearth is going out, but a mysterious fire burns on.

There is complete darkness. The bedroom door opens, and Sieglinde, in a white nightdress, enters, and quietly, quickly, walks to the fireplace. She tells Siegmund that she has drugged Hunding into a deep sleep. Siegmund must use the night to save himself. Excitedly, he says that he is saved by her presence. She then tells him how she became Hunding's wife by force, and how, as she sat sadly at the marriage ceremony, the sword was implanted in the tree by a stranger, an old man with his hat pulled down over one eye. The Valhalla motif (7) tells us who this was. Only the man who should be worthy of it would be able to pull it out of the tree, Then, in growing ecstasy, she says that she knew that only a friend and deliverer would win the weapon and free her from her bondage and distress. Embracing her passionately, Siegmund declares that this friend has come and has fallen madly in love with her.

At this point the main door flies open. Sieglinde starts with surprise, and pulls herself away, asking who went by, who entered. The door remains open, revealing a wonderful spring night, with the full moon bathing the lovers in bright light, so that they can suddenly see each other quite clearly. Siegmund says that nobody went but someone came: the spring has brought warmth into the room. Drawing Sieglinde to the couch beside him, he sings his spring song, telling in rapturous tones how May has vanquished winter, and Siegmund and Sieglinde have found each other; all that has kept them apart lies in ruins (27). Wagner responds to the glowing poetry of his own text with the poetry of his music. Sieglinde answers with her own ecstatic cry, 'You are the spring' and pours out her feelings of love and of affinity with Siegmund, whom she had recognized as her own from the moment she set eyes on him. At that moment she had found herself. Enchanted, she puts her arms about his neck and looks closely into his face.

With abandon, they sing of their new-found bliss, and come to realize their kinship. Pushing Siegmund's hair back, Sieglinde notices particularly the likeness between their faces and heads. Elaborations of the Wotan-Valhalla motif indicate their common parentage, and they recognize why they feel such sympathy with one another. When she asks if he was really called Wehwalt, he replies that he is no longer called that since she loves him, and declares that she should call him what she will. Carried away, she now realizes Wälse was their father, that he put the sword in the tree, and therefore this lover of hers must be named Siegmund, the victor. Jumping to the tree trunk and grasping the hilt of the sword, he triumphantly declares that he *is* Siegmund. This is the weapon promised him by his father in his hour of deepest distress. Even in this hour of victory, the shadow of Alberich's curse on Wotan falls upon the sword, bringing death in its wake, and we hear the motif of renunciation (6), but we must also note again that these motifs must not be too specifically labelled. As Ernest Newman has pointed out, this motif can be considered as referring to the love which Alberich renounced.

Now, with superhuman strength. Siegmund heaves the sword from its 'scabbard' – the tree. He shows it to Sieglinde, who is overcome with surprise and delight, and names it Notung, as the sword motif resounds in the orchestra (20). Sieglinde now tells him who she is, his own sister, whom he has won at the same time as the sword. He answers that she shall be his bride, and they will further the Wälsung race. Now the sword motif is combined with that of their love as they fall passionately into each other's arms to consummate their union. However, the orchestra has the last word: as the curtain is lowered a reminder of the Nibelung music tells us that their happiness will be brief.

ACT 2

The prelude, stormy and wild, depicts the flight of the Wäl-sung pair from Hunding's house. The sense of agitation in the music is unmistakable; gone is the blissful glow of the close of the previous act. Sieglinde is obviously in distress, with Sieg-mund trying frantically to calm her. Freia's motif of flight (9) is very much in evidence; so, soon, is the motif of the Val-kyries' call (28).

Scene 1

When the curtain rises we see a gorge in the distance below a high range of rocks, which slope downwards towards the front of the stage. Wotan, in battledress and carrying his spear, is accompanied by his Valkyrie daughter, Brünnhilde, also wearing armour. He bids Brünnhilde, in urgent terms, to prepare to fight in the combat between Siegmund and Hund-ing, and to take Siegmund's side. With her shout of joy, 'Hojotoho', she jumps from rock to rock, to a peak at the right, where she looks down into the chasm below and calls back to Wotan to prepare for a battle himself as Fricka is in view. As she looks as though she is coming to pick a quarrel, Brünnhilde deems it best to get out of the way. She disappears behind the mountain tops. Fricka rides from the gorge on to the ridge in a chariot drawn by two rams (neither the chariot nor the animals are ever seen in modern productions). She quickly dismounts and advances menacingly to where Wotan stands at the front of the stage.

Wotan hails Fricka's appearance with anything but pleas-ure, for he knows through experience that her arrival will mean the old storms and troubles, yet he must submit.

Fricka approaches Wotan in a dignified manner. Although she is censorious, even vindictive, she is not wholly unsym-pathetic. In her role at this stage of the drama, as protectoress of marriage, she is convinced of her case, and even when she is seen in the moral climate of today, she is not wholly unjust in her condemnation of Wotan's inconsistent behaviour. She has been listening to Hunding's complaints and, as guardian of wedlock, she demands punishment for the impudent pair who have defied social morality. Wotan, in answer to her remonstrances, declares that he does not hold sacred the oath that binds together those who do not love each other, and advises her to bless the bond of the lovers. That aggravates Fricka even further; her womanly indignation now knows no bounds. She exclaims: 'It this then the end of the everlasting gods, now that you have created the Wälsung race?' She goes on, in her railing mood, to castigate him for having overthrown all that he once held sacred, for infidelity to her, for having abased himself to the extent of fathering a pair of human beings, and for living in the woods as Wolfe. She reserves a particularly fierce barb for Brünnhilde as bride of his desire, born to him through the wild love he had for Erda. Finally, he has sired this Wälsung pair by a vulgar human being, and to this litter he would now sacrifice his wife.

It is a powerful diatribe, a splendid outburst for a dramatic mezzo. Wotan, however, is quite unmoved by it. Quietly he tells her that she is unable to comprehend something that she has never before encountered. She is bound by convention, cannot see, as it were, beyond her next step, while he has foreseen the need for a hero, free from divine protection, who will be able to fulfil the present need of the gods. She retorts that he is merely trying to confuse her, and, in any case, she does not believe that a hero such as he envisages could ever exist: this is only a new artifice of Wotan's to dupe her. She reminds him that Siegmund is not that free, unprotected hero, for he owes his existence to a god and his sword. But, Wotan protests, Siegmund won it for himself in his hour of greatest need.

From this point, Wotan's whole bearing and behaviour grow more and more dejected, and to illustrate this Wagner uses a motif in the low woodwind that finely matches his state of mind (29). Seeing that she has Wotan at a disadvantage, Fricka presses home the attack with great relish, pointing out that it was Wotan himself who made it possible for

Siegmund to have the sword. At this, Wotan starts up in anger. Fricka gains in confidence, declaring that she will at least defend the rights of marriage, and saying that surely Wotan does not want her to be insulted by a victory for Siegmund. Gloomy and defeated, Wotan asks what she wants. Don't protect the Wälsung, she commands. He agrees. But she demands more, and he submits after one more cry of protest; the Valkyrie must also forsake Siegmund.

Wotan has seen that he has deceived himself into thinking it possible to deliver Siegmund and yet to make him a free hero. If that should happen, divine law would be broken, a law established by the god himself. Fricka would, in that case, have to give place to the offspring of a mortal woman. Such a defeat would bring ridicule on the gods, or so she believes. Wotan is compelled to acknowledge the logic of Fricka's case, and so swear an oath that Hunding shall triumph.

Fricka forces this course on Wotan only after Brünnhilde's return. The Valkyrie stops quickly when she sees Fricka and slowly leads her horse down the rocky path, stabling it in a cave, while Fricka delivers her exordium, a rather complacent lyrical passage in which she majestically orders Wotan to bid Brünnhilde withhold aid from Siegmund. It represents convention triumphant. As he gives Fricka his promise, Wotan throws himself down on a rock in terrible misery and inner anger. Fricka sweeps imperiously off, stopping briefly in front of Brünnhilde, saying that Wotan has a message for her. She gets into her chariot (should she have one) and quickly drives away.

Scene 2

Brünnhilde sees her father sitting motionless with his head in his hands, lost in gloom and walks over to him. Letting one arm fall disconsolately and his head sink on to his breast, Wotan comments in a choked voice that he has been caught in his own trap; he is the least free of all beings. Brünnhilde comments that she never has seen Wotan like this and wonders what is gnawing at his heart. He now becomes more and more anguished until he cries out frighteningly to the effect that the gods are in distress and shamed. His anger will never end, his misery is eternal, he is the saddest of beings. Brünnhilde, terrified, throws down shield, spear and helmet, and kneels, solicitously, at Wotan's feet, begging him to tell her of his distressing troubles; she then rests her head and hand lovingly in his lap. After gazing for a long time into her eyes and caressing her hair, he emerges from his thoughts and says that if he were to tell her everything he might lose his own hold upon his will. Brünnhilde, in the softest, most sympathetic tones, reassures him that she is indeed his will, a part of himself. Before he begins his long narration he says that whatever he says is for her alone; it is as if he were talking to himself.

Wotan gazes steadfastly into Brünnhilde's eyes, and in a voice stifled and full of fear, he begins his story. He tells Brünnhilde of his longing for power, and of the treaties and laws he made in order to acquire that power. He goes on to tell how Alberich had forsworn love to win the Rheingold, how he, Wotan, had taken the Ring from Alberich and paid for Valhalla with it instead of restoring it to the Rhine. In this recapitulation of *Das Rheingold* he shows how wrong he had been in allowing Alberich to act as he did and then taking advantage of those actions.

He now relates how Erda warned him of the curse attached to the Ring, how he sought her in the bowels of the earth, in order to learn wisdom, how he gave her his love, how she, Brünnhilde, and the other Valkyries are the fruit of that love, and how they had brought him the spirits of heroes fallen in battle. Brünnhilde interjects that they have indeed filled his hall with a multitude of such heroes. What else troubles her father? The real danger, as he sees it, is that Alberich may succeed in his sworn ambition to reclaim the Ring, in which case Valhalla would be lost, and all Wotan has created would be set at naught. He speaks of his dilemma: he wishes to get back the Ring himself from Fafner, who now guards his treasure, but because of his bargain with the giant he cannot bring himself to attack him. Thus he is powerless, fettered by his treaties. At this we hear the motif of his distress (30) on the cellos. His plan, as he has already suggested to Fricka, is to bring on the scene a hero, free of the gods' influence and power, who could reclaim the Ring on his own account. How, he asks, can he bring into being this liberating agent, one who, while defying him, will be most dear to him? What a predicament for a god, what a terrible disgrace! Once again, in powerful, distressful terms, he expatiates on his own state of mind. Brünnhilde now quietly inquires whether Siegmund does not, in fact, act on his own? Wotan does not answer directly, but comments that he had wandered through the woods with him, and made him bold. Now, however, he has only the sword for protection and (this is said heavily and bitterly) Fricka had unerringly discovered what he intended to do, and has now forced him into his present disgraceful position. Will he then, Brünnhilde asks, deprive Siegmund of victory? In a passage where Wagner graphically illustrates Wotan's anguish, the god admits that he must now murder that which he loves and betray the one who has trusted him. Now, his suffering turning to despair, he invokes in the most urgent terms the ruin of the gods, 'the end, the end', and for that end Alberich is unceasingly working. For Erda had told him that when a child, the fruit of hatred, should be born to Alberich, the end of the gods would indeed be at hand. Wotan has now heard that a woman whom Alberich bought with his gold has borne him a child while he, who wooed with love, not with money, has not been able to beget a free man. Then, in the most biting, angry terms, he blesses the Nibelung boy and bequeaths to him the empty glory of the gods.

Shocked, Brünnhilde asks what she must now do. 'Fight for Fricka,' he says bitterly, 'and for marriage vows'. For the first time in her existence, she does not seem in accord with her father's wishes. Wotan, she says, is fighting against himself in deciding to favour Hunding against Siegmund. The love he bears for the latter, Wotan has instilled into Brünn-hilde's heart also, and now she, too, must fight against Sieg-mund. She is incredulous, and fails to show obedience to Wotan's wishes. Only when he threatens her with his wrath, that she, the instrument of his will, should be rebelling against him, does she reluctantly gather up her arms after her father, frustrated and despairing, has stormed away into the mountain crags. She muses to herself that her weapons have become heavy now that she knows to what use she must put them, and it is with a slow, sad step, instead of her usual buoyancy, that she walks towards the back of the stage. When she reaches the mountain peak, and looks down into the valley, she catches sight of Sieglinde and Siegmund. She watches their approach, then walks to the cave where her horse is tethered and disappears from view.

Scene 3

Siegmund and Sieglinde come into sight on the top of the mountain. Sieglinde, hurrying ahead, is restrained by Sieg-mund. She wants to push further on. Embracing her gently and firmly, Siegmund tries to calm her, and briefly succeeds. She gazes passionately into his eyes and embraces him. Sud-denly she is off again, in the grip of a nameless terror, full of self-reproach. She entreats him to leave her, declaring that she is dishonoured and has brought dishonour and shame on him. Her anguish is truly reflected in her jerky and unsettled vocal line. Even in the most blissful moments of their love she felt that she was under a curse. Siegmund replies that Hund-ing shall pay for bringing disgrace upon her with his life when Notung devours his heart, and the horns of the pursuers are heard in Hunding's sinister rhythm.

Starting up once more in terror, Sieglinde says that she can hear their furious echoing all round. Dissonances in trumpets and horns aptly reflect her terrified state. She can see the dogs and men howling for blood. As if crazed, she looks vacantly ahead, asks where Siegmund may be, and beseeches him not to shun her. After once more throwing herself on him and then rising, terrified, she says she now sees the dogs rushing on Siegmund to pull him to pieces. One further cry to Siegmund and she falls fainting into his arms. After making sure that she is still alive, he holds her carefully and lets her head rest in his lap. They remain thus until the end of the next scene. He bends over her and kisses her tenderly.

Scene 4

Brünnhilde, with horse and armour, comes slowly out of the cave, walking solemnly forward. When still some distance from Siegmund she stops to look at him, then moves forward again. When she is very close to him she stops. In one hand she holds her spear and shield; with the other she leans against the neck of her horse, looking gravely at Siegmund as the sombre chords of the death motif resound on trumpets and trombones (31). It is noble and grief-laden, like Brünnhilde herself, when she begins by calling Siegmund's attention to her presence. She then announces to him the approach of death. Siegmund looks at her earnestly and questioningly before asking her whither she wishes to lead him. When she says that it is to Valhalla, he inquires whether he will find his father there and whether he will be welcomed by a woman. To both questions she answers that he will, but when he asks whether Sieglinde will come too, Brünnhilde says that she will not: she must still breathe earthly air. At this, he leans tenderly over Sieglinde, kisses her forehead, and quietly tells Brünnhilde to greet Wotan and his fair daughters, but that he will not follow her to Valhalla, for he must remain where Sieglinde has her being.

Brünnhilde insists that he must die, be killed by Hunding. All his protests about the power of his sword are in vain: he who made it for Siegmund has taken away its power. When he hears this, Siegmund bids the Valkyrie be silent while he gently caresses Sieglinde once more, and cries shame on him who gave the sword. Brünnhilde becomes deeply moved by his sorrow and love, and she is touched that the delights of Valhalla mean so little to him. She promises to protect Sieglinde, but Siegmund will not grant that right to anyone but himself: sooner than leave Sieglinde, he will kill her. At this he draws his sword, and points it at his loved one. In a violent outburst of sympathy and unable to bear her own attitude any longer, Brünnhilde declares that they shall both live; she will turn the tide of battle in Siegmund's favour. His utter helplessness and misery have inspired her with a pity akin to love, and in her compassion for the unhappy pair she has forgotten Wotan's commands and his fury. Hunding's menacing horn-calls are heard again off-stage. She orders Siegmund to prepare himself and tells him his sword will be true. Taking her horse, she hastens into a ravine on the right. Siegmund gazes happily and with dignity after her as the stage darkens, thunder clouds hiding the mountains. The horn calls draw nearer. The whole of this scene, known as The Annunciation of Death, has a solemn, slow-moving gravity and beauty all its own.

Scene 5

Once again, Siegmund bends over his beloved to see if she is breathing. As the sweet sound of his love song is faintly recalled in the orchestra, in one of the work's most tender passages, he bids the seemingly lifeless figure sweet dreams. The horns become more insistent, and Siegmund commands Sieglinde to sleep until the battle has been fought and peace has returned. After kissing her gently and lowering her lightly to the ground, he stands up resolutely, draws his sword and disappears over the summit of the mountain in a flash of lightning.

Sieglinde begins to move restlessly in her dreams, as she remembers the scene in her childhood when strange men carried her out of her burning home. She calls for help to her brother, and then is awoken by a flash of lightning and a terrible clap of thunder. She stares ahead with growing terror as she watches the storm, hears Hunding's call, and Siegmund's reply. A sudden flash of lightning reveals the forms of the fighting men. With all her strength she calls to them to halt their fight. She rushes to the pass but another flash breaks over the two men, making her reel back as though blinded. The Valkyrie motif (32) announces Brünnhilde's arrival on the scene. She is seen hovering over Siegmund and guarding him with her shield. Just as he is aiming a fatal blow at Hunding, Wotan appears in a growing red light and stands over Hunding, holding out his spear. He peremptorily orders the splintering of the sword. Brünnhilde has drawn back at the sight of Wotan, leaving Siegmund unprotected. Now Hunding thrusts his spear into the breast of his defenceless enemy, and Siegmund sinks, dying, to the ground.

Sieglinde has watched this scene with breathless anxiety. As she sees Siegmund fall, she utters a cry and, throwing herself on the ground, remains as if lifeless. Darkness covers the scene once more. Brünnhilde can dimly be seen running towards Sieglinde, whom she succours in her arms. She recovers the broken pieces of the sword, and disappears with the half-unconscious woman, on her horse. The clouds lift, and Hunding can be seen pulling his spear from Siegmund's chest. Wotan, ringed with clouds, stands behind him on a cliff. He leans on his spear as he sadly contemplates the body of his hero. Then, waving his spear, he contemptuously orders Hunding to go and kneel before Fricka, and announce to her that Wotan has avenged the insult offered to her. At Wotan's gesture Hunding falls dead. As the motif of Wotan's spear peals out in the orchestra (8), the god breaks out in wrathful exclamations against Brünnhilde's disobedience and resolves that her punishment shall be terrible. Amid thunder and lightning, he disappears, and the motif of distress (29) closes the eventful act.

ACT 3

The third act opens with a piece of graphically descriptive music, known as the Ride of the Valkyries and often played separately as an orchestral work. It is dominated by the Valkyries' motif (32) indicative of spirit and energy, and depicting their galloping, panting horses. It is a powerful prelude, wild and grand in concept.

Scene 1

When the curtain rises, we see the top of a mountain, with pine trees on the right. To the left is the entrance to a rocky cave, which looks like a natural hall. Above, the rock rises to its highest point. At the back, the view is clear. Rocks, some high, some low, form the edge of a precipice, which should be imagined falling away steeply in the background. Cloud formations scud across the ridge of rocks, as if driven by the storm. Gerhilde, Ortlinde, Waltraute and Schwertleite, four of the Valkyries, in full armour, are assembled on the rocks around and above the cave, looking out for the arrival of their sisters, Helmwige, Siegrune, Grimgerde and Rossweisse. They hail each other, one after another. In between flashes of lightning, the others arrive, with dead warriors at their sides. They greet each other, laugh, wave their spears, and indulge in joyous war-cries, while they leave their horses in the wood.

Brünnhilde alone is absent. Suddenly Siegrune, on watch, espies her, riding furiously towards the height, and carrying a woman instead of a dead hero. As Brünnhilde dismounts in the wood, the others hurry to her, inquiringly. They return with her, supporting and guiding Sieglinde. Far from being elated, she is in deep distress and implores their aid in protecting her and Sieglinde from Wotan's wrath. He is following her, and Ortlinde and Waltraute point out the storm clouds coming up from the north, announcing the approach of the god. Brünnhilde hastily tells them what has happened. The Valkyries, in utmost consternation, are astonished at her disobedience. She implores one of her sisters to lend her a horse so that Sieglinde can escape, but the Valkyries, being conformists, are unwilling to invoke Wotan's further anger. Sieglinde, who until now has been staring gloomily and blankly ahead of her, gives a start as she is embraced by Brünnhilde. She says that she does not want to be saved now that Siegmund is dead, and begs Brünnhilde to plunge a sword into her heart. But Brünnhilde bids her live for

the sake of the hero whom she will bear, the pledge of Siegmund's love. Terrified at first, Sieglinde afterwards reacts with
sublime happiness and implores Brünnhilde to save her child.
The clouds grow blacker, the thunder rolls nearer, as Brünnhilde raises Sieglinde and urges her to escape, while she herself
awaits Wotan's anger. But where shall she go? After discus-
sion, Siegrune suggests a wood to the east where Fafner, now
changed into a dragon, guards the Ring in a cave. It may be no
place for a pregnant woman but Wotan shuns it. Bidding
Sieglinde be brave, Brünnhilde gives her the remnants of the
sword for her son, Siegfried, who will forge them anew. At this
the motif to be identified with the hero of the rest of *The Ring*
is first heard (33). With great emotion, Sieglinde cries out her
thanks to Brünnhilde, the most glorious of women, to a motif
which will be heard later at the close of the whole cycle (34).

She bids Brünnhilde farewell and hurries away to the
woods. The mountain top is now covered with dark thunder-
clouds as the storm increases in force. Wotan's approach is
off-stage commanding Brünnhilde to halt. At first she watches
Sieglinde's flight. Then she returns anxiously to the centre of
the stage. Her heart sinks as she hears Wotan's fury, and she
implores the Valkyries to shield her. They run in fear to the top
of the rock, pulling Brünnhilde with them and hiding her in
their midst. Looking anxiously to the woods, they see a fierce
light, indicating Wotan's approach. All else is dark.

Scene 2

At last he enters, in a towering rage, and strides up to the
Valkyries at the summit, searching for Brünnhilde. They try to
soften his resolve to punish her, but their entreaties are useless.
Of them all, she alone was party to his innermost thoughts;
none knew his will as she did. Now she has broken the bond
that existed between them. She has openly scorned him. She
must not shirk her punishment.

On hearing this, Brünnhilde steps forward voluntarily, in
humility, and comes within a short distance of Wotan. She tells
him to pronounce punishment. The music aptly mirrors her

chastened state. Wotan tells her that she has herself shaped her sentence. His will has brought her into being, and now she has acted against it, she can no longer be a Valkyrie, but must become a mere mortal. Wagner shows how deeply Wotan has been offended by the passion with which he expresses his sentence of excommunication. No longer will Wotan send her from Valhalla's halls to bring to him the chosen heroes; no more will she hand him the drinking horn at the gods' solemn banquets; no more will she receive his caresses. She is cut off from the gods, rejected by the immortals; she is banished from his sight.

At this, the Valkyries become greatly agitated, crying 'Woe'. Brünnhilde herself asks if Wotan indeed intends to take from her all that he once gave? No, he replies, but he who over-powers her here on the mountain top, where he intends to leave her defenceless and asleep, to him shall she henceforth belong. In vain the other Valkyries beg Wotan to revoke the sentence; in vain they cry that the shame will affect them, too. Wotan becomes only more wrathful; their faithless sister is banished from their midst; no longer will she ride freely with them. She will become an ordinary house-wife, doomed to sit by the fire and spin, the object of universal derision. Brün-nhilde falls to the ground with a cry. The Valkyries recoil from her in horror. the god then commands the other Valkyries, if their sister's lot terrifies them, to shun her, and never to offer her comfort or consolation, or they will share her fate. With more cries of misery, they separate and disappear into the woods. Thick cloud settles on the face of the cliff. Tumult is heard in the woods, and a flash of lightning shows the Val-kyries, crowded together and riding off with loose bridles. Gradually the storm subsides, and during the following scene there is calm as twilight falls and night comes.

Scene 3

Wotan and Brünnhilde, lying prone at his feet, are now left alone. During a long, solemn silence, neither stirs. At length she raises her head. Beginning timidly but gradually gaining in confidence, she asks if the crime she committed was so shameful, so dishonourable that it needs to be punished with shame and dishonour. Raising herself slightly, she begs Wotan to moderate his anger and explain what hidden guilt has caused her to be exiled. It is an appeal expressed so movingly that it begins to work on Wotan's soul, but at first he asks only that she should question herself as to her own guilt. She replies that she knew that Wotan had loved Siegmund and had been forced by Fricka to destroy his favourite hero. In doing so he was his own enemy. Moreover, she had seen what he had seen, Siegmund's sorrow and despair. Her compassion for the unfortunate Wälsung knew no bounds, and she had realized that Wotan had tried to hide from himself that he really wished for Siegmund's victory. The love that filled her heart was truly at one with his for the Wälsung. The god replies that she should not think love's bliss so easily attainable. What torment had it cost him when he was unable to see his way clear to save Siegmund. Since she has taken love and life so lightly, let her see how she can fare away from him, from his innermost thoughts and wishes. In opening out his whole heart to his once beloved daughter, he shows how close she really is to him still. His musing is tender and compassionate, at least until he decides that they must part.

She quietly answers that she was only loving what he loved and that, as she is part of him, in dishonouring her, he brings shame on himself as well. Unrelenting, he declares that as she has followed the power of love, she must now submit to the man who shall compel her to love. She now begs that if she must leave Valhalla, he who wins her may at least not be a worthless coward, but Wotan says he cannot choose for her. The more resolute he seems in his attitude, the more urgent become her appeals. She then reminds him, to his fury, of the Wälsung, who owe their origin to the god himself. Wotan silences her, and will not give in to her wishes; he will not protect the fruit of Sieglinde's womb. When she reminds him of the sword, he breaks out in anger again. He will hear no more; she must submit to her fate. Nevertheless, it is evident that he has been touched by her appeals.

He now decrees, to a new motif (35), that her punishment is to sleep, defenceless, until someone wakes her and claims her as his wife. Falling on her knees, she implores him that she should at least have some protection, so that only a fearless hero may claim her. Obviously moved, Wotan says that she asks too much. Clasping his knees she entreats him further not to be so cruel as to condemn her to such a vile disgrace. With wild exaltation, she suggests to him that a fire should surround the rock on which she is to lie.

At last softened and convinced by her appeals, Wotan turns impetuously to Brünnhilde, raises her to her feet and gazes with emotion into her eyes as he breaks out into his great farewell, to a mighty outpouring of sound in the orchestra, Wagner echoing the deep feeling of his character and opening the lyrical floodgates. The thoughts of Wotan and Brünnhilde have at last become one. After she has declared in impassioned terms that a bridal fire shall surround her until one freer than Wotan releases her, Brünnhilde sinks on his breast, moved and exalted. As he holds her in a long embrace and she gazes gravely into his eyes, he bids her a fond farewell, saying that he is looking into her eyes for the last time. For his final, tender words he cups her head in his hands: 'So the god departs from you; so kisses he the godhead away!'

He imprints a long kiss on Brünnhilde's eyes. She sinks back, gradually becoming unconscious in his arms, while he supports her to a mossy bank. There he lays her down under a broad fir-tree, gazes at her, closes her visor. After gazing longingly at her again, he covers her with her shield, walks slowly away, turning to take one last look. Then, walking solemnly to the middle of the stage and pointing his spear at a large rock, he summons Loge to conjure a magic fire with which to encircle it. Now the magic fire motif flickers in the orchestra (36).

As Wotan strikes the rock thrice with his spear and calls more urgently on Loge, a flame issues from the rock. Wotan is surrounded by bright, flickering fire. The god passes the point of his steel all round him and as the fire gradually spreads until it blazes at the edge of the mountain, the chromatic fire motif courses through the orchestra, contrasted with the sweet, peaceful sleep motif (35). At Wotan's words: 'he who fears the point of my spear shall never pass through the fire', Siegfried's motif (33) is heard. At this Wotan stretches out his sword in conjuration. After casting one more glance back at Brünnhilde, he slowly moves away and disappears in the fiery glow. The sounds, too, die away into silence.

As with all the other separate parts of *The Ring*, *Die Walküre* has a mood and character all its own. Whereas *Das Rheingold* was primarily expository and dramatic in concept, and concerned itself with the intrigues and trickery of the dwarfs and gods, *Die Walküre* moves paradoxically on to at once a lower and higher plane of activity, lower in the sense that the first act is mainly a human drama, higher because its subject is love and passion expressed in the most ardent terms. Wagner knew, of course, about illicit affairs and loveless marriages so that the Sieglinde/Siegmund and Fricka/Wotan relationships, as portrayed in two marvellously contrasted dialogues, represent opposite poles of dramatic and musical expression. Wotan's great monologue in Act 2 takes the work on to yet another plane, one of deep psychological insight into a single character, a character *in extremis*, an immortal creature wracked with the pains and frustrations of mortal beings. Again we find Wagner sympathizing absolutely with a character while he is writing for him, both vocally and orchestrally, in a manner that transcends anything that had existed in music to that date. Far from being merely recapitulatory or boring, this narration, when fully comprehended, is one of the peaks of *The Ring* as a whole.

The succeeding colloquy between Brünnhilde and Siegmund (the Announcement of Death) brings together a godly and an earthly figure. In it, Brünnhilde is eventually touched, to some of the most tender music in the cycle, by his purely human love for Sieglinde and forced by it to disobey her father's express command. The fourth and final dialogue in *Die Walküre* – and the most affecting – is that in Act 3 between the infuriated god and his erring daughter, his *alter ego*, the personification of his will, who gradually and movingly persuades him to relent his anger towards her.

Die Walküre is an opera full of telling orchestra music in which Wagner attained the absolute mastery of his new-found method of development through motifs. He uses instruments, too, with a wonderful appropriateness to situation: the onomatopoeic evocation of a storm at the start in the strings, the fierce brass that accompanies Wotan's anger, to harps at the point where Brünnhilde promises Siegmund *Wunschmädchen* (desirable women) if he will only submit to death and entry into Valhalla, the power released in the Ride of the Valkyries, the dejection expressed in bass clarinet and cor anglais when Brünnhilde lies prostrate before Wotan, the magnificent release of different kinds of impassioned music for the earthly love of Sieglinde and Siegmund in Act 1 and for the love of Wotan for Brünnhilde in his great farewell.

The work requires noble singers: a powerful yet lyrical soprano for Brünnhilde, a tender soprano for Sieglinde, a dramatic mezzo for Fricka, a baritonal *Heldentenor* for Siegmund, a tremendous bass-baritone with lyrical possibilities for Wotan. With such a cast and a great conductor in the pit, *Die Walküre* is still probably the most overwhelming experience for most people in *The Ring* cycle.

Siegfried

ACT 1

The prelude to *Siegfried* immediately tells us that we are once
again in a different world and that some time has passed since
the events of *Die Walküre.* Immediately the sly, frustrated
figure of the dwarf Mime, last encountered in the third scene of
Das Rheingold, is brought before us by the appearance of the
motif of reflection in the bassoons (37). Its dark, sinister
colouring at once tell us that Mime is up to no good. The
recollection of the Ring (5) and sword (20) motifs show what it
is the dwarf seeks to attain. With these are intermingled the
motif of the Nibelung's servitude (13) or Alberich's triumph so
that by the time the curtain rises we are well informed about
his thoughts.

Scene 1

We are at Mime's home in the depths of the forest. This is a
cave in the rocks. It stretches right back of the stage on the left,
only three-quarters of the depth of the stage on the right. It has
two entrances towards the forest, one to the left, another,
broader, to the right at the back. On the left, against the cave
wall is a great forge shaped from the rock face; only the
bellows are man made. The chimney, naturally formed, goes
up through the roof. Nearby are the necessary tools, a big anvil
and other blacksmith's implements. As the curtain rises,
Mime, to the sound of the Nibelung's anvil motif (11) on the
strings, is hammering impatiently at a sword beside the anvil.

At length he stops, obviously out of spirits. He utters a bitter complaint that all his work is in vain, because the best sword he can make is a mere plaything in the hands of Siegfried for whom it is intended. At this he crossly throws the sword on the anvil and slumps on his elbows. Only one forged from the the broken pieces of his father Siegmund's sword would be unbreakable, but all his skill as a smith will not help Mime to forge that. Leaning back, still deeper in thought, he muses that with such a weapon Siegfried would be able to kill Fafner, the dragon, and thus reclaim the treasure, which the creature is guarding in his den. We hear the onomatopoeic dragon motif heave up in the orchestra (38). Once more he sets to work in the utmost dejection, wailing that all his effort is in vain, because he knows the lad will snap his best effort in two, and again he lets the hammer drop from his hand. Now, to the accompaniment of a motif describing the young, bounding Siegfried (39), the youth enters, dressed in rough forest clothes, a silver horn hanging on a chain at his side. He rushes in exuberantly, with a bear which he has on a rope. With boyish high spirits he sets it on Mime. Siegfried laughs loudly; Mime, terrified, drops the sword and flees behind the forge. Siegfried makes the bear chase Mime all over the place. Mime shrieks for Siegfried to get rid of the animal. The bear, Siegfried says, has come to coax the sword out of Mime. When he hears that the sword is finished, he gives the bear a slap on the rump with the rope and lets it go. The animal lopes off into the forest. Mime emerges, trembling, from his hiding place and tells Siegfried that he does not mind him killing bears, but bringing them into the home is going a bit far. The boy says that he has been looking for a better companion than the one sitting at home, and he preferred this growling bear, who came out of the woods at the sound of his horn. Mime now gives him the sword. Siegfried snatches it from the anxious dwarf and smashes it on the anvil and the pieces fly everywhere. Mime shrinks in terror. Siegfried, although he is spirited and naively innocent, undoubtedly has a streak of ferocity in him, as can be seen and heard as he now vents his spleen on Mime, saying that

Das Rheingold
Scene 3: Wotan and
Loge capture Alberich

Das Rheingold Scene 4:
The entry of the gods into
Valhalla

Die Walküre Act 1:
Siegmund and Sieglinde
with 'Nothung'

Die Walküre Act 2:
Brünnhilde tells
Siegmund he must go
with her to Valhalla

he has lost patience with him, and were he not a silly old gnome, he might melt him down along with his forge. At this he flings himself angrily down on a stone. Mime cautiously keeps out of the boy's way, retorting that he is always ungrateful and forgets what Mime has done for him. Siegfried is unimpressed and turns his back crossly on Mime. Going over to his pots on the hearth, the dwarf coaxingly suggests that Siegfried might like some meat and soup. The petulant boy knocks pot and meat out of Mime's hand. He says that he can well look after himself where food and drink are concerned. Taking up an aggrieved stance and whining, Mime reproaches him, and reminds him, to a motif signifying his complaining (40), of how he warmed and fed him as an infant, gave him toys and a ringing horn, and now he sits at home slaving for Siegfried, while the latter roams in the forest to his heart's content. All the thanks he gets is Siegfried's hatred – and he starts to sob. When Siegfried turns round and gazes at Mime, Mime carefully avoids his look.

Siegfried replies that the dwarf has, in truth, taught him much, but one thing he has not taught him, and that is how to appreciate Mime. He hates the sight of the dwarf, and with great vehemence, he expresses his dislike, declaring that he would love to make an end of him. All the birds and beasts of the forest are dearer to him than is Mime. How comes it, then, that he returns to Mime's dwelling? Still keeping his distance Mime replies that this shows how deear to his heart Siegfried is. Shrinking still further away from the boy, Mime says that Siegfried's wildness is to blame and he must control it. The young always yearn for the nest and here, for the first time, Wagner brings a note of true feeling into this score (41). Siegfried cannot help but love his Mime, who teaches and tends him. Hardly taking notice of what Mime has been saying, Siegfried comments that he has heard the birds sing happily in spring, seen them pair and bring up their young ones; likewise the deer, foxes and wolves. Thus, he has learned what love means, and he asks Mime where his wife may be. Ignoring a peevish intervention from the dwarf, Siegfried presses home

his questions with the highly awkward one for Mime: how did
he make Siegfried without a mother? Greatly embarrassed,
Mime replies that he is father and mother in one. Siegfried cries
out that that is a lie: young things resemble their parents, and
he has seen his own image in a brook, and knows that he looks
no more like Mime than a shining fish looks like a toad. Mime
crossly tells Siegfried that he is talking arrant nonsense. Siegfried is undeterred. Asking why he returns to Mime's lair, he
answers his own question by saying that it is because he must
find out from the dwarf about his mother and father. Seizing
Mime by the throat, he says that if necessary he will force out it
of him.

Mime makes a gesture and nods his head to signify that he
will tell all, and the youth releases him. After again chiding the
boy for his ingratitude, Mime starts to relate what has happened. It is true, he says, that he is not Siegfried's father, nor
indeed any relation. Out of pity he has sheltered the ungrateful
boy. To the motif that indicates the Wälsungs' sorrow, he tells
how, long ago, he had found a woman weeping in the forest,
how he helped her into the cave, tended her, how she gave
birth in distress, then died. Siegfried sorrowfully asks if his
mother had died because of him? While he remains deep in
thought, Mime answers that she gave him the babe to protect.
Then he starts up his old cry about how he brought up the boy,
but is cut short by Siegfried: this is the name by which, the
dwarf says, his mother had said that he should be called.
Siegfried then asks his mother's name. Mime tries to evade the
question, but eventually reveals that it was Sieglinde. But, in
reply to another question, he says that he never knew the name
of Siegfried's father: he knows only that the man was killed.

Once more the dwarf attempts to begin his plaint again, but
Siegfried tells him to stop and to give proof of this story. Mime,
after a pause for thought, produces the two fragments of the
broken sword, saying that Siegfried's mother had left him
these, the remains of the sword which his father had carried in
his last fight, and the sword motif is heard, quietly, in the
orchestra (20). Elated, Siegfried immediately realizes that it is

from these that Mime must forge a new sword, and he promises that he will have the dwarf's scalp if he does not do the job properly. With the sword, Siegfried will go out into the world, far from Mime, and be as free as the birds of the air or the fish of the sea. A motif expressing this free life (42) accompanies his joyful utterance, and he rushes off into the forest, leaving Mime wondering, as he goes to sit down again behind the anvil, how he can hold the boy, repair the steel, and weld the needed sword. He slumps down in despair on the stool behind the anvil.

Scene 2

The Wanderer (Wotan) enters slowly from the forest by the back door of the cave. He is wearing a long, dark-blue cloak, and carries a spear as a walking-stick. A large hat with a broad, round rim comes down over his missing eye. A slow motif, expressive of dignified strength, represents Wotan as the Wanderer (43). It is intoned by the brass. His quiet self-possession contrasts markedly with the frightened, inhospitable way in which Mime receives him. Approaching slowly a step at a time, he asks for the favour of Mime's house and hearth. He tells the dwarf that the world calls him Wanderer, and that he has travelled much. In that case, Mime says, he should hurry away from here. The Wanderer replies that men have always benefited from his wisdom. The dwarf protests that he is wise enough, and is in no need of thinkers, spies or loiterers. The Wanderer is not so easily put off. He comes ever closer and eventually seats himself near the fire in spite of Mime's protestations, and offers his head as a forfeit if he cannot answer to Mime's satisfaction any questions that the dwarf may put to him.

Mime, who has been gazing open-mouthed at the Wanderer, is now frightened and says to himself that, in order to get rid of this loiterer, he must question him cleverly. Out loud he agrees to the Wanderer's proposition, stating that he will put three questions. He first asks what race inhabits the depths of the earth. The Wanderer replies that it is the Nibelungs, ruled over by Alberich, who had amassed great treasure by means of the magic Ring; appropriate motifs are heard in the orchestra. Then, sunk in still deeper thought, Mime asks what race inhabits the face of the earth, and gets the reply that it is the giants, whose home is Riesenheim. Two of them, Fasolt and Fafner, gained the Ring, but conflict broke out between them over the spoils and Fasolt was slain. Fafner, transformed into a dragon, now keeps guard over his treasure. Again the fitting motifs are heard in the orchestra. Now completely carried away by his dreams, Mime asks what race lives on the cloud-covered heights. To the majestic Valhalla theme (7), Wanderer-Wotan replies that there dwell the gods. Licht-Alberich, Wotan himself, the *alter ago* of Schwarz-Alberich, is the lord of the gods, and governs the world by means of a spear cut from the primeval ash-tree's sacred branch. The Nibelungs have bowed before him; the giants have been tamed; and as he strikes his spear, as if accidentally, on the ground, a soft thunderclap is heard. Mime shrinks back in terror. So, the Wanderer asks, has he given true answers and freed his head from forfeit?

In answering the third of Mime's questions, we feel that, for the first time, Wotan has put into words his realization that he and Alberich are the light and dark side of a single nature, and he cannot command Alberich any more than he can command the giants.

Having won his wager, Wotan has earned the right, by the laws governing such things, to ask Mime three questions. Mime is frightened but he masters his nervousness and hesitation, and prepares himself. In mock modesty he derides his own knowledge, but he will do his best. The Wanderer asks on what race (we hear the Wälsung motif) Wotan wrought his wrath, although he loved it more than any other on earth. Mime replies that he knows little about heroes, but that question he can answer: the Wälsungs. To Wälse were born the wild twin-pair, Siegmund and Sieglinde. Siegfried was their offspring. The Wanderer genially compliments him on his knowledge. One question he has answered correctly; here is the second. A wise Nibelung is tending Siegfried, who must kill Fafner for him. With what sword shall Siegfried fight Fafner? Mime feels that this is almost ludicrously easy to answer. Stimulated by the subject, he rubs his hands in glee, and replies that Notung is the name of the glorious sword, struck in the ash-stem by Wotan. Only Siegmund was valiant enough to withdraw it, and he carried it into battle until it was shattered into fragments by Wotan. These are now looked after by the wily smith, who knows that only Notung can slay Fafner in the form of the dragon. Delighted, Mime asks if he has saved his head a second time.

Wotan laughs and says that Mime is the wittiest of wise men, but if he is so clever, can he answer the third question which is: who will make the sturdy sword anew? At this, the dwarf starts up in terror. He cannot answer that question, for it is the very thing he himself wants to know. In a fit of despair, as if crazed, he hurls his tools about, and cries out that he does not know who will weld the sword, how the miracle will be worked. Calmly rising from the fireplace, the Wanderer comments that he has answered three questions put to him by the . dwarf about pointless topics, whereas Mime might have asked things which would have been of use to him. Now he has not understood the answer or saved his head, but the Wanderer will leave it to be hacked off by the one who has not learnt fear, who shall forge Notung anew. Mime stares at him as he turns, smiling, to go, into the forest. The dwarf is now more terrified than ever, and collapses on to his stool behind the anvil.

Scene 3

Mime, left alone, stares in front of him into the wood, and falls into a panic. Trembling violently, he wonders what these flames are, striking out at him. He imagines, in his terror, that he perceives the gaping jaws of Fafner chasing after him, and the orchestra throughout this imaginative passage vividly depicts the menacing, flashing lights of Mime's nightmare, and his vision of the monster. As Mime collapses in terror behind the anvil, Siegfried returns, and the mood changes immediately as he demands to know how the forging of the sword has gone. He enters the cave, and stops short in astonishment at not seeing Mime. At his call, however, a feeble voice answers from behind the anvil. On hearing that Siegfried is alone, Mime creeps out, looking dishevelled, and asks how he can make the sword. Thrown into confusion he repeats half to himself the words of the Wanderer: that only one who knows no fear will be able to make the sword again, and Mime's head will be forfeit. Siegfried is impatient, uncomprehending. Gradually gaining control of himself, Mime realizes that he must teach Siegfried what fear means, and after Siegfried has shaken him in exasperation, Mime begins his attempt to teach him fear. Approaching the puzzled Siegfried with increasing familiarity, he tells the boy that Sieglinde, his mother, had made him promise never to let her son go out into the world without knowing what fear is. 'Is it an art?' the boy inquires brusquely. Then comes a thrilling, graphic description from Mime and the orchestra of the nature of fear – a buzzing and roaring that seizes one's whole being, making the body burn, the heart burst with its pounding.

To Siegfried, it seems an exhilarating sensation, and he asks Mime how he can learn it, and how a coward can be his master. Mime replies that he will lead him to Neidhöhle, at the east end of the wood, where there is a dragon (38) that has killed and eaten many. He assures Siegfried that it is not far from the world, where the boy longs to be. Siegfried agrees to go once the sword has been forged. Mime once more bewails the fact that he has been unsuccessful in that task. Siegfried brushes the dwarf aside, and strides to the hearth to begin the work himself, heedless of Mime's remark that if he had diligently applied himself to learn forging, it would now be useful to him. Siegfried replies that when the master does not know his job, there is not much chance of the pupil learning from him. He cocks a snook at Mime, then tells him not to interfere or he may well fall into the fire.

Siegfried piles a large quantity of coals on the hearth and keeps the fire going while he fixes the fragments of the sword in the vice and files them into shavings. Mime watches him, and from time to time offers words of advice which are contemptuously rejected. Eventually Mime is astonished at the success of the boy's unorthodox ways. All this is set to music portraying the prodigious energy and sweat of the action. By now Siegfried has heated the forge to its height, and while he continues to work with furious force, Mime begins to think of his dreadful dilemma: if Siegfried kills Fafner, and does not learn fear, Mime's head will fall by Siegfried's sword. On the other hand, if Siegfried does not kill Fafner, Mime cannot acquire the Ring. By now Siegfried has filed the fragments away to powder and put them in a crucible, which he sets on the forge fire. Arousing Mime from his unpleasant reverie, he asks what is the name of the sword. On being told that it is Notung, Siegfried fans the fire and begins his forging song (44) to an accompaniment in the orchestra that vividly describes the burgeoning fire. As the bellows blow and the fire roars, Mime hits on what seems to him a brilliant idea. He will prepare a beverage for Siegfried which he will offer the boy when he is tired and thirsty after grappling with the dragon, and which will cause him to fall into a deep sleep. Then Mime can kill him with Notung and take possession of Ring and treasure. He rubs his hands with pleasure at the prospect of his coming triumph, and mocks the absent Wanderer for thinking him silly. Meanwhile, Siegfried continues with his work and his song. He pours the glowing contents of the crucible into a mould, and holds it aloft, before plunging it into a water trough. Steam and loud hissing rise from it as the steel cools. Now Siegfried thrusts it into the fire and works energetically at the bellows; his growing exuberance is reflected in the orchestra.

Where Mime is concerned the thought is father to the deed and he begins to prepare a deadly potion from the contents of various jars. Siegfried keeps a wary eye on the dwarf, putting his drinking pot on the opposite side of the fire from Mime's, and the counterpoint of Siegfried's forging and Mime's brewing continues to the end of the act. Hypocritically, Mime congratulates Siegfried on his skill at the forge. From now on he shall do the smithing, while Mime boils eggs. However, the boy is justifiably suspicious of the dwarf's cooking and vows to touch nothing prepared by him. He now takes the mould out of the fire, breaks it and lays the glowing steel on the anvil. Now, to a vigorous new motif (45), he rains blow upon blow on the steel and exults in his work. At last he completes it and brandishes the blade in the air before plunging it again into the water. He fastens the blade into the hilt while Mime, busy with his bottles downstage, works himself into a frenzy of delight as he imagines himself lord of the world and, more particularly, master of Alberich. Having hammered the rivets into the handle, Siegfried picks up the finished sword and cries out 'Notung' triumphantly. His paean of praise to the new-forged weapon ends as he first raises it and then brings it down on the anvil, which splits in two and falls apart with a resounding crash. Mime, who has jumped on his stool in a transport of delight, now topples down in terror as Siegfried exultantly holds the sword aloft.

ACT 2

The prelude to the second act immediately announces that it is to be of very different character from the first. Over string tremolandos and a suggestion of the giants' music, the cumbersome motif of Fafner as a dragon heaves itself up menacingly from the depths of the orchestra (46) while through the prevailing gloom echoes of the Ring motif (5), the curse motif (17) and the servitude motif (13) are heard, thus preparing us for Alberich's presence when the curtain rises.

Scene 1

We are in the depths of the forest. The ground rises from front to back where there is a little knoll, from which it descends to a huge cave, only its upper mouth visible to the audience. Through the trees on the left is a rough cliff. It is a dark night, the gloom being impenetrable at the back. Resting against the cliff face, brooding gloomily, is Alberich, keeping his unholy watch by Fafner's den. To the accompaniment of the annihilation motif (16), he tells us that he has been watching and waiting without cease to reclaim Ring and treasure. Will this be the day? He becomes aware of a wind from the forest, from where a bluish light is gleaming. Can this be the approach of the dragon's assassin? No, the light fades as quickly as it appeared, but out of the darkness the Wanderer approaches, suddenly visible in a shaft of moonlight. Alberich recognizes his adversary.

Bursting out in rage, Alberich tells the shameless thief to be off. His behaviour contrasts with the calm authority of Wotan as Wanderer; he replies that he has come to observe, not to take part. Alberich is not pacified and Wagner puts into his mouth a magnificent indictment of the god's behaviour. He is not as stupid now as when he was previously tricked by Wotan and forced into giving up the Ring. He knows that the god cannot himself take away the Ring from the dragon, because he is bound by treaties and will lose the power of his spear. Alberich now reminds him of these facts in demoniacal joy at the thought of the anxiety that Wotan feels about the fate of the Ring and the fear he has that it may land once more in Alberich's hands. Wanderer, with a certain sophistry, points out that it was not by treaties that he subdued Alberich, but by the naked power of the spear itself. Alberich sees through that one, declaring that Wotan's bold words mean nothing: he is obsessed by fear of what will happen to those who inherit treasures which are accursed, and is even more fearful that they may fall once more into Alberich's hands. So, he shouts, with powerful scorn, Wotan must tremble at the thought that Alberich may rule the world.

Still calm and enigmatic, the Wanderer replies that he who wins the Ring will control the world. Alberich immediately thinks of Siegfried, the hero Wotan has created for that express purpose. No, says Wanderer, turning away from Alberich's scornful tongue, it is not he, Wotan, with whom Alberich must pick a quarrel, but Mime who is bringing the boy here, unknowing, to gain the prize for himself. Siegfried is his own master, will stand or fall by his own strength and means, so Alberich only has Mime to worry about. Alberich is greatly relieved, for he believes he can cope with his despised brother and the uncouth boy. Alberich's other questions are turned away: all the Wanderer will say is that the hero will get the treasure. But perhaps it would be a good idea to warn Fafner of the approaching danger; then he might give up his toys. At this the Wanderer stands at the mouth of the cave and calls to the dragon to awake. Alberich shows some alarm at this, and wonders what the madman is doing. From the depths at the back, Fafner's voice emerges (coming through a loudspeaker). He asks who is disturbing his sleep. The Wanderer calls out that someone has come to warn him of trouble, and Alberich corroborates this by saying that a strong hero is approaching to attack Fafner. The dragon merely replies that he is hungry. Alberich then tells him that it is only the Ring that the hero wants; if Fafner will let the Nibelung have it, he will prevent the fight, and the dragon can go on guarding the treasure and live in peace. Fafner answers with a complacent yawn: 'What I have I hold; let me sleep.'

At this, the Wanderer laughs and says that Alberich's stroke has misfired. He adds confidentially that everything works to its appointed destiny, and that nobody can alter the course of fate. With these parting words of warning, the Wanderer disappears quickly into the forest, and at his departure the wind blows and the light shines as they did at his approach. Alberich gazes at him as he rides away, saying that, laugh as he will, he will see the gods' downfall, and Alberich himself triumphant in the end. He slips into the cleft at one side of the stage, and as the day dawns, the stage is empty. During this entire scene, Wagner weaves the appropriate motifs in and out of the texture with even greater mastery than in the past, almost as if their appearance were inevitable in that particular place.

Scene 2

As day breaks, Mime and Siegfried enter. Siegfried is wearing
his sword on a belt made of bark rope. Mime reconnoitres the
land warily; he investigates the background, which still lies in
deep shadow while the knoll in the foreground becomes a little
brighter. Then he addresses Siegfried, saying that they have
reached the appointed place. Siegfried, sitting under a great
lime tree and looking round him, asks if it is here that he will
learn what fear is, adding that if he does not, he will continue
his wanderings by himself and at last be rid of Mime.

Sitting down opposite Siegfried, so as to keep an eye on the
cave, Mime assures him that if he does not learn fear here, he
will hardly do so anywhere else. He points out to Siegfried the
dark hole where Fafner lies hidden and describes to him the
awe-inspiring size and horrible jaws of the beast. When Siegfried says that he will close up the dragon's mouth, Mime adds
that it drips poisonous venom. 'I'll avoid that,' says the boy.
Then Mime vividly describes the snaky tail which will crush
Siegfried's limbs as if they were glass (an odd simile perhaps in
view of the work's timelessness). Siegfried declares that he will
defend himself from that. All he needs to know is where the
dragon keeps his heart. Is it where others have it? Being told
that it is, he sits upright and says that that spot is where he will
plunge Notung. Then he asks whether that is what fear is
about. Mime tells Siegfried to wait until he sees the beast; then
he will lose his senses and his heart will quake with fear. He
will then know how much Mime loves him.

'You shall not love me!' is Siegfried's retort. 'Get out of my
sight!', and once again he menaces the dwarf with force. Mime
decides to leave him, to await the issue of the combat at a
nearby stream, but Siegfried laughingly suggests that he will let
the creature go there to quench his thirst on Mime, who tells
the boy to call on him if he needs refreshment after the fight.
Siegfried, with an impatient gesture, motions to the dwarf to
leave, which the latter proceeds to do, uttering at the same time
the wish, aside, that Siegfried and Fafner may destroy each
other. He then disappears into the wood.

Siegfried lies down comfortably under the lime tree to a dreamy, tremulous movement from the lower strings, which represents forest sounds. All the woodland seems to be coming to life under the influence of the sun. Siegfried has sunk into a dreamy mood. He thinks of his parents, wondering what they were like. Certainly his father must have been like himself, for if Mime had a son, would he not be just as grizzled and grey, as small and crooked, as the dwarf and go limping along in a similar fashion? The very thought of Mime makes Siegfried angry. However, he leans back and for some time looks up into the branches in silence while the forest continues to murmur. Then he reflects tenderly and with great inwardness on what his mother must have been like, her eyes soft like a doe's, only much more beautiful. He wonders if all human mothers die at the birth of their sons. He then wishes, to a quiet, but yearning accompaniment, that he could see her, his mother, a human woman. This is all the more moving as human affection has not as yet been any part of his life. He sighs quietly, leaning still further back, and the forest sounds grow more distinct. A bird is heard in the oboe, flute and clarinet, capturing Siegfried's attention. He listens with increasing interest to the bird-song.

He muses on what its message may be. If only he could understand it! The old dwarf had told him that there was meaning in the song of birds. He meditates for a moment. His glance falls on a reed bush not far from the lime tree, and he tries to imitate the bird, and perhaps be understood by it. He runs to the nearby stream, cuts a reed with his sword, and shapes it into a pipe. He cannot successfully imitate the song: after a few vain and discordant attempts, he gives up in despair. But he soon smiles at his failure, realizing that learning from the little bird is not easy. Instead he throws away the reed, and determines to try his silver horn. He takes it from his hip and blows on it a vigorous, well-sustained call, looking up expectantly on the sustained notes to the bird (motifs 33, 39). As the happy tune reaches its climax, something stirs at the back of the stage. It is Fafner in the shape of a monstrous, serpentine dragon, arising from his lair. He bursts through the undergrowth and lurches to the higher ground, reaching it just as he gives out a loud yawn. Siegfried looks at him in astonishment, commenting that at last his tune has brought forth a sweet comrade. The orchestra depicts the clumsy menace of the dragon. When Fafner asks what is there, Siegfried replies that if this is a beast who has learnt to talk, maybe he can learn fear from it. Emitting a loud laugh, Fafner says that he wanted a drink, now he has found food too, and he opens his jaws, showing his teeth. For a while they taunt each other, and Fafner threatens the youth with his tail. Eventually Siegfried draws his sword and lunges at Fafner, who lurches further up the hillock, spouting venom. Siegfried avoids it, gets closer and to one side, where Fafner tries again to reach him with his tail. Just as he is about to reach the boy, Siegfried leaps over him and wounds him in the tail. Angered by the blow, Fafner rears up the front of his body, intending to crush Siegfried with his whole weight. In doing so he lays his breast open and Siegfried, quickly sensing where the dragon's heart is, plunges in his sword up to the hilt. Groaning with pain, Fafner raises himself even higher, then collapses as Siegfried releases his sword and jumps out of the way.

In a weak voice, Fafner inquires, to the accompaniment of his own motif (38) and that of annihilation (16), who is the bold boy who has done the deadly deed. The boy replies that he knows nothing. All he can say is that the monster has provoked him into combat. Fafner now proceeds to tell him, accompanied by the appropriate motif, how he was once a giant and killed Fasolt, becoming master of the accursed gold; how he changed himself into a dragon to guard the treasure; and how he has now fallen at the hand of the boy. He also warns him that whoever set Siegfried on to him is plotting Siegfried's own death. Siegfried says that the giant's dying words seem wise, and tells Fafner who he is – Siegfried. Fafner repeats the name, sighs, rears up, and dies.

'Dead men tell no tales,' comments Siegfried, so his sword must act as his guide. Fafner had conveniently rolled on to his side as he died, and so Siegfried can now pull his sword out of the dragon's breast. In doing so he smears his hand with blood. He hurriedly draws it back and involuntarily puts his fingers in his mouth to suck the blood from them. As he does this, his attention is increasingly drawn to the song of the birds, and suddenly he realizes that he can understand the meaning of their song. One of them on the lime tree tells him that the Nibelung's treasure is now his. The Tarnhelm will be useful to him: the Ring will make him master of the world. Thanking the bird for its good counsel, he descends into the dragon's lair and is lost to view.

No sooner has Siegfried vanished into the cave than Mime slinks in, looking carefully about him to make sure that Fafner is dead. Alberich also trots in from his hiding place, watching Mime closely. Mime moves cautiously towards the cave, but Alberich bars his way. The scherzo that follows is one of Wagner's most brilliant flights of characterization as the two break out into angry exclamations of hatred and defiance. Each is naturally bent on getting the Ring, which each considers as his own property – Alberich because he stole the gold in the first place, then made the Ring, Mime because he has brought up Siegfried in order that the youth might acquire the Ring for him. After they have quarrelled for some time, Mime proposes a division of the treasure. All he wishes for is the Tarnhelm: that is only fair, seeing that he made it; Alberich may have the Ring, and the rest of the gold. Alberich, with a mocking laugh, scorns this proposal. The Tarnhelm, indeed: he would not have a peaceful night's rest with Mime up to his tricks. Alberich tells him that he will not let him have anything. Mime then works himself up into a great state, and screams: 'Then is nothing to be mine?' In that case, Alberich shall have neither Ring nor Tarnhelm, because Mime will summon Siegfried to his aid.

At this inconclusive point of their argument, Siegfried comes out of the cave. The dwarfs notice that he has chosen the Tarnhelm and the Ring. Alberich curses at this. Maliciously, Mime calls on him to make Siegfried give up the Ring: then it will soon be Mime's. At this point he slips away into the wood.

Alberich, muttering that, before long, the Ring will return to its rightful master, disappears into a cleft in the rocks. Siegfried, who has been pondering over his new toys, now pauses on the knoll in the centre of the stage. He has not the slightest idea of what use they can be to him – we hear the Rhinemaidens' motif (2) as symbolic of this unknowingness. All they are to him are souvenirs of his victory over Fafner, or, as Robert Donington puts it, 'having seen mysteries greater than he can yet understand and treasures richer than he can yet put to use'. He puts the Tarnhelm in his belt and the Ring on his finger. Peace again reigns in the forest; the murmurs grow louder, and, almost involuntarily, Siegfried notices the bird again and listens with bated breath. The bird tells him not to trust Mime or listen to his flattering words. What the dwarf is really plotting in his heart Siegfried will be able to discern through having tasted the dragon's blood. Siegfried's look and actions show that he has fully understood the bird. As he sees Mime approaching, he keeps quite still, leaning on his sword, observant and withdrawn on the knoll, and does not move throughout the following scene.

Mime slinks in, and observing Siegfried downstage, mutters to himself that perhaps the youth has already encountered the Wanderer, who may have told him some tale. He must therefore be at his most cunning, and delude the obstinate boy. Deceitfully, he approaches Siegfried, and a masterly scene begins, full of subtle characterization. Throughout, Mime more or less speaks what he thinks rather than what he really intends Siegfried to hear. Feigning friendliness all the time, he declares that Siegfried has now accomplished the deed for which Mime brought him up, so the dwarf intends to give him a potion that will close his eyes in eternal sleep. Mime will then take possession of the Ring. He goes on to say that he has always hated the young hero and his race, and while Siegfried was making the sword, prepared a fatal beverage. Now he wants that sword for his own purpose. Somehow confused as to what has been thought and what has been speech, Mime becomes peeved when Siegfried interprets his words too literally, but then returns to his amiable mood and tries to persuade the boy to take the cordial. Alberich says ruefully that he would be glad of a healthy drink. Joking happily, as if describing the state of cheerful intoxication the juice would induce, Mime tells Siegfried to drink, and as he lies unconscious Mime will hack off his head with the sword. Mime chuckles with delight at the prospect. When Siegfried asks whether then Mime intends to murder him when he is asleep, Mime is again vexed. 'Have I really said that?', he asks. Then, in his most coaxing vein and apparently showing concern for Siegfried's well-being, he repeats his intentions in other words, declaring that he is after the treasure and must be rid of the boy. He pours the juice into a drinking horn and once more presses it on Siegfried. Filled with a sudden fit of violent revulsion, Siegfried kills Mime with a single blow. Alberich's mocking laughter is heard from the cleft in the rocks.

Siegfried, looking at the body, replaces his sword and declares that Notung has paid the wages of hatred. He heaves Mime's body to the cave mouth and pushes it in. Then he rolls the dragon's corpse into the mouth of the cave so as to block it completely. Together, he says, they can guard the glittering treasure. For a while he gazes thoughtfully into the cave, then slowly comes forward. It is midday. He wipes his hand across his forehead. He says to himself that he is hot and tired from all his hard work and from the burning rays of the sun, so he lies down in the shade of the lime tree and once more gazes up through the boughs. He watches the birds as they hop from branch to branch, and fly after each other; they all delight in love, but he is lonely. He has neither brother nor sister; his mother is dead, his father slain in combat. How he longs for a companion, for someone to love. He asks the birds to help him. Looking sadly up into the tree, he seeks good advice and receives it. The Woodbird tells him that the loveliest of women lies asleep on a high rock. If he can go through the flames surrounding her, then Brünnhilde will be his. A great surge in the orchestra is based on a motif representing Siegfried's yearning for love (47).

At the good news, Siegfried springs impetuously to his feet, thanking the bird for its sweet song. A desperate longing, which he hardly understands, has taken possession of him, and he feels that he must get away from the forest and up to the rocks. The bird warns him that only he who knows no fear can pass through the flames. Siegfried exclaims that he has not been able to discover what is fear, even from Fafner. Now he is burning with desire to learn that from Brünnhilde. The bird hovers for a while, teasingly, leading him in different directions, but eventually takes the exultant Siegfried towards the back of the stage – towards his goal.

ACT 3

The prelude depicts the unrest in Wotan's soul by means of a subtle combination of the motifs associated with him and his actions. After the long period that elapsed between the composition of Acts 2 and 3, Wagner's command of his musical means gained in confidence and economy. This prelude, at once urgent and compact, closely developed in the most cogent terms yet used by Wagner, is indicative of the new strength in the composer's writing.

Scene 1

The curtain rises on a wild landscape at the foot of a rocky mountain, rising steeply to the left, near the back of the stage. The Wanderer enters. He moves deliberately to the cavernous mouth of a cave in a rock downstage. There he places himself, leans on his spear, and calls to Erda to awake. He chants an invocation to the goddess of the Earth, immortal woman, and conjures her to arise from the subterranean depths. He says he is singing a waking-song to the eternally wise woman.

The cave-mouth grows brighter with a bluish light. Very gradually Erda emerges. She appears to be covered with hoar; her hair and clothes throw off a shimmering light. She declares that she is powerfully drawn by the call, and has awoken from her sleep of knowledge. Who is it who has disturbed her? To a recurrence and interplay of the motifs appropriate to his narration, Wotan describes who he is and why he has come to visit her. He has travelled the world seeking primeval wisdom, but only she has it. She knows what is hidden in the depths, what relates to nature and the elements, because she is everywhere, her mind is attuned to all things, and he needs her definitive advice. She replies, cryptically, that her sleep is dreaming, her dreaming brooding, her brooding the management of wisdom; but while she sleeps the Norns are awake, busy weaving the rope – the thread of destiny (as we shall see in the prologue to *Götterdämmerung*). They gently spin what she knows. So, for wisdom, Wotan should seek the Norns.

He answers that they spin according to an inexorable law; they can reverse or alter events; but he would like to know from her how to stop a revolving wheel. She again fails to enlighten him. Human deeds cloud her mind. Once she was conquered by a master (Wotan, of course) and bore him a wish-maiden. Let him find her and discover her mind. He asks if it is Brünnhilde to whom Erda is referring. She has flouted his will. The stubborn girl has dared attempt what he had wanted to do but had refrained from doing. For her presumptuous action she has been suitably punished and lies fast asleep, only to awaken when a man woos her for his wife. Would it help to question her?

Erda broods on this for a while, and there is a silence before she speaks again. She resumes by saying that she has been dazed since she awoke: the world seems confused to her. Is it true that, while she slept, her Valkyrie child was sentenced to an unguarded sleep? Is he who taught defiance now punishing defiance? Is he who thought up the deed, angry now that it is done? Does he who upheld truth now shun it and govern by breaking oaths? In that case, she wishes to descend again and let sleep once more seal her wisdom.

The anxious Wanderer will not let her depart. Once she had implanted care's sting into Wotan's daring heart: warned of him of his shameful downfall. How now can he conquer his anxiety? Again Erda answers in riddles, declaring that he is not what he calls himself. Why did he come so turbulently to disturb her peace? He, too, now speaks elusively, telling her she is not what she thinks she is. The earth-mother's wisdom will come to an end; her knowledge will end. Does she realize what he intends? After a long silence, he explains that as she is unwise, her ears must be opened so that, carefree, she can sleep forever. The god's downfall is at hand, and it no longer grieves him because it is now what he wishes. Once, in despair, he had resolved on a plan that he is now happy to carry out. At this declaration a new motif, whose notes ascend the scale with quiet but impressive grandeur is given out (48). This represents Wotan's bequest to the world: it is noble because it will be associated with the coming of a better world. In rage and loathing, he says, he had presented the world to the hateful Nibelung; but now his inheritance is bequeathed to the glorious Wälsung, chosen by him, although the youth does not know it. The brave boy, unaided by the god, has gained the Nibelung's Ring. His innocent, noble nature will cripple Alberich's curse. Erda's child, Brünnhilde, child of joy and wisdom, will be awakened by the hero; she will then redeem the world. So Erda can go back to sleep and watch Wotan's downfall. To the ever-youthful hero the god is delighted to yield – and he commands Erda away to everlasting peace. This whole passage, one of the most overwhelming in the entire cycle, is further evidence of Wagner's mature command over the development of the relevant ideas into new skeins of sound.

As it comes to an end, Erda closes her eyes and, after gradually sinking into the earth, disappears completely. Meanwhile the cave has become quite dark. Moonlight illuminates the stage; the storm has subsided.

Scene 2

As the second scene begins, the Wanderer walks towards the cave and leans with his back against the rock, his face turned towards the front of the stage. He declares that he sees Siegfried approaching; he is prepared for the final turn in events which he dare not, cannot control. He remains by the cave as Siegfried's bird flutters to the foreground, singing its carefree tune. Suddenly it stops, flies anxiously back and forth, and swiftly disappears into the background. As Siegfried enters from the right, he comments that his bird has flown off, having done its duty, and has left him to find his own way to the mountain. He starts off towards the back, when the Wanderer addresses him, asking where he is going. Siegfried stops, turns round and says that perhaps the person who just spoke will direct him. He walks up to the Wanderer and says that he is looking for a rock surrounded by fire: a woman sleeps there and he must awaken her.

The Wanderer asks who gave him this information and who made Siegfried desire her. A bird of the forest who gave good advice is the reply. Disbelievingly, the Wanderer says that a bird twitters but no man can understand it. How was Siegfried able to make sense of its message? That was through the blood of a savage dragon, which he destroyed at Neidhöhle. It had hardly wetted his tongue when he began to divine the bird's message. Now, in answer to the Wanderer's questions, Siegfried recounts the story of his life, how the deceitful Mime had wanted him to learn fear, how he slew the dwarf with the sharp sword that he himself had forged: he cannot tell who made the pieces of the sword in the first place, only that had he not forged them anew, they would be useless. The Wanderer chuckles good-humouredly and says that that would also be his opinion, too. He looks approvingly at Siegfried.

Surprised, Siegfried asks what this old inquisitor is laughing about. In some impatience he asks the Wanderer to stop delaying him unless he can point the way onwards. The Wanderer reproves him, tells him to be more respectful (throughout this scene Siegfried is quite unaware what he owes to the god). Even more irritated, Siegfried bursts out that he has been bothered by one old fellow. Now that he is rid of him, he may take similar measures against the Wanderer if he continues in the same vein, and he makes an appropriate gesture. Then he goes nearer to the Wanderer and asks him why he wears a big, droopy hat over his face. The Wanderer replies that it is his custom when he walks against the wind. Inspecting him still more closely, Siegfried comments on the missing eye, no doubt plucked out when the old man had stood in somebody else's way. The Wanderer's grave reply is that, though the youth knows nothing, he knows how to look after himself. Then he declares that with his missing eye, Siegfried himself is looking at the remaining one. The subtlety of this observation is lost on Siegfried, who laughs irreverently, and once more asks to be shown the way. Speak, he demands, or he will send the Wanderer packing.

Quietly and lovingly, the Wanderer reproves the impudent boy and asks to be spared his abuse. He is painfully grieved by the youth's threats. He has loved Siegfried's kind, but has scourged it in his fury. He does not want that anger to be aroused today: it could ruin them both. Siegfried pays no heed to him, and once more demands that the Wanderer get out of his way; his bird has told him how to find the sleeping woman. As it becomes darker again, the Wanderer bursts out in anger that the bird flew away to save its life; it saw here the lord of the ravens and it will suffer if they catch it. The youth must not take the way it suggested. Stepping back in surprise and defiance, Siegfried asks who is the Wanderer to stop him. The Wanderer replies that Siegfried should fear the guardian of the rock. The sleeping girl is imprisoned by his power. A sea of fire surrounds her. Whoever desires her must brave the blaze. At this he points to the rock's summit, and while, in a magnificent passage, he demands that Siegfried look towards the smoke and flames, a glow of firelight is to be seen, growing brighter all the time. The Wanderer tells Siegfried that he will be eaten up by the fire. Excitedly, Siegfried declares that he must go to where the blaze burns, to Brünnhilde.

As he moves forward, the Wanderer bars his way, saying that if Siegfried does not fear the fire, his spear will block the youth's path because it is the symbol of mastery and the sword Notung was once smashed by it – as it will be again. He stretches out the spear, at which Siegfried shouts that he has at last found his father's foe, and can exact a glorious revenge. He will shatter the spear in pieces with his sword. With a blow the deed is done: the spear is broken in two. A flash of lightning comes from it and travels up the fell to the heights, where the glow grows in brightness. A clap of thunder is also heard, but quickly dies away. The fragments of the spear fall at the Wanderer's feet. He quietly gathers them up and, giving way, sadly remarks that Siegfried should go on. He, the Wanderer, cannot prevent him. He disappears at once into total darkness. Thus, Wotan's power is annulled; he will no more play an active part in the drama. The primal order writ on his spear is no more. A new order, forged by Siegfried and Brünnhilde, must come to pass.

Siegfried now comments that, with his spear shattered, the coward has departed. He sees the sea of flame as it shines down the mountain. With the bird's message still in his ears, he knows that he must brave the wonderful flames that rise so radiantly before him. He will bathe in the fire, and there find his bride, a companion to love. Siegfried, blowing his horn, plunges into the fire, which sweeps down from the summit. Gradually he is lost to view as he moves towards the summit. The blaze reaches a climax, and then slowly dies down as the rosy light of dawning day appears. In the first part of this interlude, Siegfried's horn call cuts through the orchestral tissue; then, as the fire sinks down, the sleep motif (35) goes through various transformations and is enmeshed with other motifs.

Scene 3

As the last scene of the opera begins, the clouds gradually begin to thin and dissolve into a fine reddish mist. This divides, part of it floating away to reveal a bright blue sky bathed in daylight, part appearing at the edge of what is now seen to be the rocky summit, the setting for the final act of *Die Walküre*. In the foreground lies Brünnhilde under the broad-boughed fir tree. She is in full, bright armour, her helmet on her head, her long shield covering her. As the orchestral sound dies away to almost nothing, Siegfried, reaching the edge of the summit, is visible at first only from the waist upwards. For some time, he gazes in astonishment at the scene before him.

Softly he declares that this is a blessedly wonderful and deserted height. He then climbs right to the top and, from a precipice at the back, he surveys the scene, still with astonishment. He looks into the fir forest and steps towards it. He asks himself what it is that is there, lying asleep in the shadow of the trees. Advancing slowly, he stops in amazement as he catches sight of Brünnhilde and wonders at the glittering steel. He thinks he might still be dazed by the fire. He walks towards her, and considers picking up the shining armour. He lifts the shield and sees Brünnhilde's form, although her face is still mostly covered by her helmet. He imagines her to be a man in armour and is impressed by the glorious head, which he thinks might be eased by taking off the helmet.

He carefully unfastens it and removes it from the sleeper's head. Brünnhilde's long locks of hair fall loose. Siegfried, startled, exclaims at her beauty. Unable to take his eyes off her, he goes into a poetic rapture at the shimmering clouds, the heavenly lake, the gleaming sun, laughing as it beams through the clouds. Now, as he bends over the sleeping form, he listens to hear if she breathes, and wonders whether to break the breastplate. He tries carefully to loosen it, then calls upon his sword for assistance in cutting the iron. With gentle care he cuts the chainmail on both sides of the breastplate. He lifts it off, and the shin-pads with it, and Brünnhilde, in soft, women's clothing, is revealed. He starts up terrified and alarmed, crying out that this is no man. A new motif depicting his confusion now becomes dominant in the orchestra (49). He gazes at the sleeping form with the utmost excitement. His whole being seems to burst into flame and a look of perturbation crosses his brow as he says that he is dizzy. In the greatest anguish he asks who will save him and invokes his mother. After falling, almost in a faint, on Brünnhilde's bosom, he raises himself, sighing. How can he wake the girl? How make her open her eyes? And when they do open, would not the sight

of them blind him? Is he rash enough to dare? As he is swaying
dizzily, he wonders if he is experiencing fear at last, and he
again invokes the mother he has never seen. Then, to a phrase
of particular eloquence, 'Im Schlafe liegt eine Frau' (a woman
lies sleeping), he realize that this sleeping woman has taught
him to fear, and he determines to find the courage to awaken
her. As he approaches the sleeping form, her appearance once
more fills him with tender feelings. He comments that her
flower-like mouth is quivering sweetly and her breath is warm
and fragrant. He calls on her desperately to awake, holiest of
women. As he gazes at her, he observes, plaintively, that she
cannot hear him. In an urgent voice, he declares that he must
suck life from those sweet lips, even if he should die in doing
so.

He falls as if dying on to the sleeping form, and with his eyes
closed he presses his lips to hers. Brünnhilde opens her eyes.
Siegfried jumps up and stands looking at her. She rises slowly
to a sitting position, raises her arms in a silent greeting to the
earth and sky now that she can see them again. As she does so,
the orchestra echoes her feelings with phrases that seem to
ascend skywards, with long, sustained chords on harps and
violins, finally forming the motif representative of her awakening (50). Solemnly she hails sun, light, radiant day. She has, she
says, been asleep a long time. Now she has awoken. Who is the
hero who has done this deed? As the brave Siegfried motif (33)
is heard, Siegfried – deeply moved by her look and voice –
stands as if rooted to the spot, and declares that it is he who has
fought his way through the flames and loosened her helmet.
Brünnhilde, now sitting upright, greets gods, world and shining earth. Siegfried, to yet another new motif, bursts out into a
transport of delight (51). He pours blessings on his mother and
on the earth that fed her (he presumes that Brünnhilde is, in
fact, his mother). The radiance of her eyes makes him happy.
With deep emotion Brünnhilde now responds with a paean to
Siegfried, who has awakened her to life. Both are lost in ecstasy
as they look at one another. She exclaims that if only he knew
how he, joy of the world, had been loved by her. He was all her

thoughts, all her cares, fed tenderly by her before he was born. All that time her shield protected him. Quietly, shyly, he asks in a rhetorical manner whether his mother is not, then, dead. Was she only asleep? Smiling and stretching out her hand in a friendly way, Brünnhilde tells him that his mother will not return. They are as one if he will love her. She then tells him that she had not realized until now that she had flouted Wotan's will because she had to fulfil his secret desire; for that she was punished. Her disobedience, she now divines, arose from her love for Siegfried.

But Siegfried cannot understand all this. He feels only the burning desire of the present, the passionate, human love with which her beauty and the sound of her voice have inspired him. With fear, she has captured him and bound him in fetters. He demands that she should stop making him fearful. He is still greatly excited and casts longing looks on Brünnhilde. She gently turns her head to one side and glances towards the fir trees. There she spies Grane, her trusty horse: he, too, has awoken, and she sees how glad he is to graze once again. Siegfried, without moving, continues to speak of his passion – for her lips, her eyes. But she now points to her weapons, which have caught her attention, and she suddenly realizes that she no longer wears her armour and so is defenceless; Siegfried tells her that he came through burning fire without shield or helmet, but the hot glow has left a burning passion in his breast. As he tries to seize her, she springs up and pushes him away with the utmost force and runs to the other side of the summit.

Brünnhilde says that she was chaste when she left Valhalla; not even the gods came near her. Heroes had humbled themselves before her. Now he has awakened her, taken away her armour and brought shame on her. She is Brünnhilde no longer. In vain Siegfried answers that for him she is still the dreaming girl. He urges her to awaken, to be his. Brünnhilde now declares that she is confused and that she doubts her own wisdom. Siegfried asks if she did not sing to him of how her knowledge was the light that led her to love him. But, looking ahead, she 'can see only darkness and bewilderment. Horror strides out and rears up over her head'. In despair she hides her face in her hands. Siegfried gently removes them, and bids her see how brightly the day shines. No, it is the day of her distress, she avers, and cries out to Siegfried to see her anguish. Then, suddenly, her look softens as a sweet thought enters her head. To soft words that she was ever herself, ever in a rapture of longing, she sings (in the minor) a gracious motif, a melody just heard on the strings (52).

The theme will be familiar to those who know the *Siegfried Idyll*, and it is to that work's second subject (53) that Brünnhilde continues with a greeting to Siegfried as the highest hero. She implores him not to approach her, not to touch her, or force her with a power that might destroy her, but to love the image of himself in her and to leave her as she is, just as when he may have stirred still water and lost sight of his reflection in the waves. Her passionate entreaties only make him love her the more. He says that a mighty waterfall streams before his eyes, and that is all he can see. He does not care if it breaks his reflection because he is now burning with a passion that cannot be cooled in the waters. He would jump in the stream, just as he is , if only its waves would blissfully enclose him and his longing would be lost in the flood. He implores her to awake, to laugh and be alive to the sweetest joys, to be his. With great emotion, Brünnhilde declares that she has always been his, and in reply he urges her passionately to be his now. The passion in him gradually takes possession of her, too. After another outburst from him in which he says that if their eyes and mouths catch fire, then she will be to him what 'in fear she was', he embraces her. By degrees the immortal in her gives way to feelings as human and agitated as Siegfried's own and she clasps him in her arms. In amazed delight, he says that, as their bloodstreams set each other alight, he has regained his courage and forgotten his fear. Wildly and jubilantly, they surrender themselves wholly to the influence of the exultant, overpowering feelings, in their hearts, although this passion bears in itself the seeds of destruction, both for them and for the gods.

Valhalla's glory can fade, the Norns break their symbolic rope, the dusk of the gods draw on, at present Brünnhilde is carried away by Siegfried's 'starlight', her own radiant love. He salutes the days, the sun, the light, the world in which she lives and with supreme cry of 'shining love' and 'laughing death' they fall into each other's arms again as the orchestea resounds to the motif of love's ecstasy (51).

Siegfried is often called the Scherzo of *The Ring*, suggesting that it is the lightest of the four dramas; in many ways it is also the most varied and colourful of the four scores, encompassing the imposing episodes where the Wanderer appears with the humorous (though often sinister) scenes with the dwarf Mime. There are also a number of jokes in *Siegfried*: Siegfried himself scores off Mime and the Wanderer, the Wanderer gains at the expense of Mime.

It is a work of great contrasts. Take the opening act. The first and third scenes, in spite of Wagner's apt portrayal of Siegfried's youthful energies, are predominantly dark and sombre in character, Wagner employing the lower strings, the bassoons and tubas to convey Mime's schemings and the louring presence of Fafner is never far away. As against that, we have the bold contrast of the central episode of conversation between Mime and the Wanderer, in which the presence of the disguised god is conveyed in warm, magisterial tones, cellos and horns being used to depict his dignity and strength.

Act 2 is notable for its representation of different aspects of nature. At the beginning we are palpably in the depths of the forest with its impression of menace and, perhaps, irrational fears, with lower instruments again to the fore. When Siegfried appears, these are dispelled and in the diaphanous episode of the Forest Murmurs, the upper strings and wind come into their own as Wagner paints an unforgettable picture of pastoral peace. That is broken by the boldly and brilliantly dramatic scene where the hero slays the dragon – *The Ring* at one of its most overtly operatic moments – and in the brisk, jerky comedy of the argument between Mime and Alberich, a vivid contrast to the Woodbird's innocent utterance. Different again in this work of almost infinite variety is the extraordinary scene where Mime's inmost thoughts about destroying Siegfried are made explicit. Once he is out of the way, the immense loneliness of Siegfried is vividly expressed in vocal line and orchestration until the Woodbird once more intervenes in radiant terms to lead Siegfried forward.

Ten years elapsed between the completion of Act 2 and the start of Act 3, a period that saw the composition of *Die Meistersinger* and *Tristan und Isolde.* When Wagner returned to *The Ring*, it was, not unnaturally, with an even greater command of his means, as can be heard immediately in the Prelude to Act 3 of *Siegfried*, where the intermingling of motifs is subtler and more coherent than ever before. It is representative of the Wanderer's troubled state of mind, and that mood is carried forward in his colloquy with Erda, whose eternal and mysterious nature is conveyed in ruminative, withdrawn music. His encounter with his grandfather, the disguised Wotan (whom he cannot recognize), contrasts the brashness of the youthful hero with the tired wisdom of the god. Once this final obstacle is cast aside, Siegfried is able to go forward unhindered in his quest. In the marvellous transition to the mountain-top, the principal Siegfried themes are integrated with the fire music, thus perfectly depicting his struggle with the flames and his triumph over them. Once on the mountain-top, the music fines away to a clear, pure texture of high strings, the very opposite of the darker sounds that have dominated the orchestra until this point and culminating in Brünnhilde's opening words, 'Heil dir, Sonne'. Primeval darkness has given way to cloudless sunshine. Triumphant C major is proclaimed as this youthful pair apparently inherit the earth and banish evil, the dark deeds of disillusion of *Götterdämmerung* still far away.

The characters themselves develop unerringly in a series of duologues. Siegfried himself has his Act 1 and Act 2 conversations with Mime, his confrontation with Fafner, and in Act 3 with the Wanderer and with Brünnhilde. The Wanderer has his question-and-answer scene with Mime and his interrogation of Erda. Siegfried is seen as a bold, somewhat unsympathetic hero but his athletic behaviour is modified by his passage of introspection (in the second and third acts) where the poetic, thoughtful side of his nature is explored, and he develops significantly in the course of the work. Mime, although he has his pathetic side (as seen in *Das Rheingold*), is undoubtedly a crafty, treacherous character who should not be played for sympathy. The Wanderer is a passive observer: indeed, at the one point where he tries to take an active part in events, it proves to be his undoing, and marks the passing of the old order.

Finally, it should be noted that *Siegfried* takes place on three significant days. On the first, Siegfried forges his father's sword; on the second day, he kills the dragon, learns what fear is, slays Mime, discovers how to make sense of bird-song, and then destroys Wotan's power. On the third, he discovers Brünnhilde and love. Mime, Alberich and Wotan, who have long foretold these events, are powerless, when they finally come about, to influence Siegfried – and the power and evil the Ring represents passes into his hands, not back to theirs.

Götterdämmerung

The Twilight of the Gods represents Wagner's original idea for a drama drawn from the Nibelung saga in *Siegfried's Death*, dating from 1848. After a doom-laden prelude, using several motifs, the new work begins, as did the former, with a scene for the Norns (three Fates of Norse mythology), daughters of Erde, begotten before the earth was created.

PROLOGUE

Scene 1

The curtain rises slowly, showing the Valkyries' rock as it was at the end of *Siegfried*. It is night. From the depths at the back of the stage a fire gleams down the mountain-side. The three Norns, tall women in long, sombre clothes, are seen. The first and oldest reclines under a broad-branched fir tree, on the right of the foreground. The second is stretched out on a rock in front of the cave. The third and youngest sits backstage centre on a rock beneath the peak. The gloomy silence is broken by the First Norn who, without moving, asks what light is shining there; the Second Norn inquires if it is already daybreak. The Third Norn says that Loge's forces blaze fiercely round the rock. It is still night. Why do they not sing and spin? The Second asks the First where she will fix the rope. The First gets up and unwinds a golden rope from herself and fastens one end to a branch of the fir tree. She says that for better or worse she winds the rope. She used to weave by the world ash-tree from whose shade a spring gushed out. From this Wotan drank. He paid a forfeit by losing one of his eyes. From the tree he broke a great branch and fashioned from it a mighty spear. That blighted the tree, and the water in the spring dried up. So the songs she sang had a sad meaning, and now she weaves no more by the world ash-tree, but fastens the rope to the fir tree.

The Second Norn receives the rope and loops it round a rock at the cave's entrance. She now tells how Wotan struck agreements and carved them on the shaft of the spear and, through them, ruled the world. A bold hero then broke the spear in battle after which Wotan sent the heroes of Valhalla to hew the ash-tree and its branches in pieces. It fell. The Third Norn now takes the rope and throws its loose end behind her. She tells how the Giants built the castle, how Wotan now sits there in state with the gods and heroes. Chopped logs that were once the ash-tree surround the hall. When that wood catches fire, Valhalla will burn and the gods will be destroyed. The rope passes once again to the Second Norn, who returns it to the First who unties it from the bough and fastens it to another branch. The First, as she looks towards the back of the stage, now asks if the day is dawning, or is the light the flicker of fire. Her sight is troubled and deceives her, but she dimly recalls the hallowed past when Loge flared up in bright flames. She asks what happened to him. The Second, winding the rope as it is thrown to her, again, round the rock, says he was subdued by the magic spear. To win his freedom, he gnawed at the notches on the spear, whose power forced him, at Wotan's command, to surround Brünnhilde's rock with fire. She also asks what happened to him. The Third, once again catching the rope and throwing the end behind her, says that one day Wotan will plunge the sharp splinters of the shattered spear deep in the heart of the fire. Furious flames will flare up, and these the gods will hurl at the heaped-up logs of the ash-tree. She throws the rope back and the Second Norn coils it and throws it once more to the First. The Second says that if they want to know when that will be, then wind the rope. Once again, fastening the rope to another branch, the First Norn comments that night is waning. She cannot see any more, nor find the strands of the rope because the threads are tangled. A blurred sight confuses and angers her mind. The Rhinegold was long ago stolen by Alberich. What happened to him?

The Second, now hurriedly and anxiously passing the rope round the cave's jagged rock, says that this rock is cutting the rope; there is no more tension in the threads and the wool is tangled. Out of 'envy and hatred' she sees the Nibelung's Ring rise. The avenging curse is gnawing through the twisted strands of the rope. What will come of this? Hastily catching the rope, the Third says the rope is too slack. It does not reach her. If she has to throw the end to the north, it must be pulled taut. She tugs at it; it breaks in the middle. Her cry that it is split is then repeated by the other two. They start up in terror and move to the centre of the stage. Grasping the broken rope, they tie their bodies to each other, and jointly declare that their everlasting wisdom is at an end. The world hears these wise ones no more. Down to their mother Erda they must go.

This scene is marked by a combination, symphonically developed, of various motifs associated with the characters and matters discussed by the Norns, with a new motif (54) holding the musical fabric together. As the rope breaks, the curse motif (17) rings out in the bass trumpet, together with other doom-laden motifs.

Scene 2

Day now dawns. The red of morning begins to light the sky. The fire continues to glow below the rock. A new theme, characteristic in its stately chords of a new Siegfried, is heard (55). So is a new motif, played by the violins, typifying a new Brünnhilde (56). The new Siegfried motif rings out with full force on the brass as the two enter. He is fully armed; she is leading her horse by the bridle. Brünnhilde addresses her hero, who she feels is longing for new adventures. One worry makes her hesitate: that in winning her, his reward was too small. What the gods taught her she has given him – but of her girlish

Siegfried Act 2:
Siegfried kills Fafner

Siegfried Act 3:
The Wanderer tries to
stop Siegfried reaching
Brünnhilde on her 'fire
girt' rock

Götterdämerung Act 1: Gutrune gives Siegfried the 'draught of oblivion' watched by Gunther and Hagen

Götterdämerung Act 3:
After the destruction of
the Gibichung hall the
Rhinemaidens reclaim their
gold, while Valhalla burns

strength and spirit the hero who is now her master has bereft her. She is now weak in wisdom but filled with love and desire. She implores him not to despise the poor creature who grudges him nothing, but can give no more. He replies that she has given him more than he knows how to keep. He asks not to be chided if her teaching has left him untaught. One piece of knowledge he does hold to, that Brünnhilde lives for him. One lesson he has easily learned, to think of Brünnhilde. They remind each other of their mutual love and devotion. Brünnhilde embraces Siegfried.

He says that he will leave her there under the protection of the fire. Then he takes Alberich's ring off his finger and gives it to Brünnhilde in exchange for her wisdom for with it is bound up his virtue. He has slain the dragon that guarded it; now she must guard it as a token of his constancy. Putting on the ring with delight, she avers that she will hoard it as her only treasure. In exchange she gives him her horse, Grane, who used to fly boldly through the air. With her it lost its mighty power; it can no longer drive its way through the clouds, but wherever he takes it, it will obey him and follow him fearlessly. She tells him to take good care of the beast and says that it will heed his words; she also tells him to speak often to it of Brünnhilde. He asks whether, through her virtue, he should go on performing deeds. She shall choose his battles, his victories will be hers. On her steed, he is no longer Siegfried but Brünnhilde's arm. They jointly declare that wherever he is, they will be together, but, she asks, will not the cave then be empty? No, he replies, because it holds them both, united. Then, with the greatest affection, she calls on the sacred gods to feast their eyes on the happy pair. Even if parted, who can separate them; separated, they will never be parted. Siegfried replies in equal ecstasy by hailing Brünnhilde as a shining star, and their voices entwine in overflowing joy.

Siegfried then leads the horse quickly over the edge of the rock, followed by Brünnhilde. Soon Siegfried and the horse are lost from sight behind the rocks as they begin to descend, and are not seen again by the audience. Brünnhilde remains alone on the promontory and watches Siegfried's descent. Siegfried's horn-call is heard from the valley. Brünnhilde listens. She goes closer to the edge and looks once more on Siegfried, waving happily to him. Her smile indicates that she is gazing contentedly on the hero as he travels blithely away. The curtain quickly falls. The orchestra takes up the horn melody, and develops it in a vigorous interlude, which has come to be known as Siegfried's Rhine Journey. It is vividly descriptive of Siegfried's descent through the flames and his journey along the river. The contrapuntal command of this passage is extraordinary.

Gradually a shadow falls across the orchestra; the Ring motif (5) and that of renunciation (6) are heard, until the sound of the music changes entirely, as hints of the dark deeds in the next scene suggest themselves. Here Wagner's art of transformation is at its most masterly.

ACT 1

Scene 1

Now the drama of *The Twilight of the Gods* begins in earnest. When the curtain rises we see the hall of the Gibichungs by the Rhine. At the back it is quite open, and we have a view of the shore leading down to the river encircled by rocky cliffs. On a throne at one side sit Gunther and Gutrune. Before them is a table with drinking vessels. On the other side sits Hagen. As Gunther calls Hagen, we hear the motif of the Gibichungs (57). He asks Hagen how his name and that of the Gibichungs now stands on the Rhine. 'It fills me with envy', replies the grim, dour Hagen. Their mother Grimhilde taught him to appreciate that. Gunther comments that it is he who envies Hagen: although he won the inheritance, Hagen has all the brains. Half-brothers' dissension was never better decided. When he asks about his reputation he is only praising Hagen's wisdom. Hagen goes on to say that although the Gibichungs' renown is considerable, there are goods they still do not have. Gunther tells Hagen not to keep the facts to himself. Hagen tells him that, in their prime, the children of the Gibichung house remain unmarried. Gunther and Gutrune are lost in thought. Then Gunther asks whom Hagen suggests that they should wed so that their prestige might be enhanced. Hagen replies that he knows a woman, the most glorious in the world. She lives high on the mountain with a fire blazing round her. Only he who breaks through the fire can be Brünnhilde's suitor, one stronger than Gunther. That bold man is Siegfried, son of the Wälsungs, Siegmund and Sieglinde. He who has grown strong in the forest would be a suitable husband for Gutrune, adds Hagen. Gutrune shyly asks why Siegfried is considered such a glorious hero. Hagen tell her that he has slain the dragon that guarded the Nibelung treasure.

Gunther now says thoughtfully that he has heard of the Nibelung treasure. Is it not of the most rare wealth? Yes, Hagen says; the man who could wield its might could make himself master of the world. Then once more Hagen say that only Siegfried can win Brünnhilde. At this Gunther rises agitatedly from his throne and strides discontenedly about the hall, asking why Hagen stirs up these doubts and discords, and makes him long for that which is unattainable. Hagen, without leaving his chair, stops Gunther with a mysterious sign as the orchestra intones the Tarnhelm motif (12), saying what if Siegfried brought home the bride for Gunther? Would Brünnhilde then not be his? Gunther turns round, again doubtful and displeased. How could that happen, he asks. Hagen answers that Siegfried might be induced to do it if Gutrune had already enthralled him. Here the orchestra breathes the motif of deceit (58). Gutrune says that he must be joking: Brünnhilde must long ago have won him. But Hagen, leaning confidentially towards Gutrune, ask her if she recalls the drink in the chest that he told her about. More secretly he tells her to trust him who got it: it will bind Siegfried in love.

Gunther has returned to the table and, leaning on it, now listens attentively as Hagen continues. He says that if Siegfried should taste the magic draught, he would straightway forget that he had seen any woman before Gutrune. He asks, then, what they think of his plan, and Gunther, jumping up, praises their mother Grimhilde who gave them this brother. Gutrune sighs with a desire to see this Siegfried. Gunther inquires how he can be found. At that very moment Siegfried's horn-call is opportunely heard, resounding joyously from some distance away to the left of the stage. He is crossing the Rhine and approaching the Gibichung castle. Hagen then turns to Gunther and tells him that the hero is roaming the earth. The world is his oyster as he restlessly hunts for new adventures. He will no doubt come to the Gibich shores by the Rhine. Gunther replies that he would be glad to welcome him, and they both listen as the horn-call offstage grows perceptibly closer. Hagen goes to the river bank, looks downstream and calls back. He declares that he can see a boat carrying a horse and a man, who is cheerfully blowing the horn. Gunther stops halfway to listen as Hagen describes how the man, with strong, easy strokes, rows the boat against the current. It can be nobody but Siegfried, slayer of the dragon.

Gunther asks if he is rowing past as Hagen hails the youth, calling across the river through hollowed hands, asking Siegfried where he is going. From the far side of the river Siegfried answers, 'To Gibich's stalwart son'. Hagen invites him to Gunther's palace. Siegfried appears by the shore in his boat and tells Hagen to moor it.

Scene 2

As the second scene begins, Siegfried brings his boat to the shore; Hagen moors it with a chain. As Siegfried and the horse jump on to the bank, Hagen gives the hero welcome. Then they are joined by Gunther. From her throne Gutrune gazes amazed and admiringly at Siegfried. Gunther offers greetings. All are silent as they look at one another. The curse motif (17) rings out menacingly.

Leaning against his horse, Siegfried stands quietly by his bark and ask which is the Gibich's son. Gunther answers he is the man Siegfried is seeking. Siegfried, saying he has heard of Gunther's fame, offers him friendship or combat in the traditional manner of the sagas. Gunther tells him to forget about fighting and to be welcome. Quietly looking round, Siegfried asks where he may stable his horse. Hagen offers to find it a resting-place. Turning to Hagen, the hero inquires how Hagen comes to know his name to which Hagen answers that he knew Siegfried by his strength. As he hands over the horse to Hagen, Siegfried tells him to take good care of Grane: there never was a nobler beast. Hagen leads the horse away to the right while Siegfried looks thoughtfully after him. At a sign from Hagen, Gutrune goes to her room to the left. Gunther moves forward into the hall with Siegfried and offers him hospitality, while a new motif, signifying their friendship, is heard (59). Gunther invites Siegfried to make free use of his father's house, to share his inheritance, his land, his people. In return, Siegfried can offer only his body and his sword. But Hagen, who has now returned and stands behind Siegfried, makes mention of the Nibelung treasure, of which rumour says he is master. Turning towards Hagen, Siegfried says that he had almost forgotten it, so little does he prize wealth, but when Hagen asks if he took nothing from it, he shows Hagen the Tarnhelm, which hangs from his belt. Hagen recognizes it as the most skilful work of the Nibelungs, and describes its magic properties. Did he not take something else? Yes, the Ring, now held by the noblest woman. To himself, Hagen mutters 'Brünnhilde'. Gunther says that for this jewel he would be giving mere baubles if Siegfried took all his possessions in exchange. He will serve Siegfried for nothing.

Hagen goes to Gutrune's door and opens it. She emerges, bearing a drinking horn, and approaches Siegfried with it. Her own sweet motif accompanies her entrance (60). She is a weak, gentle creature, caught in Hagen's web of deceit. A Gibich's daughter, she now welcomes Siegfried to the house with a drink, the draught of oblivion. Siegfried bows politely to her and accepts the horn. He holds it thoughtfully in front of him. Softly he drinks to Brünnhilde, and how ironic is his avowal that this is the first drink of true love. The orchestra breathes the motif of deceit (58), followed by that of Gutrune (60). By this stage in *The Ring*, Wagner has achieved absolute mastery in the interweaving of motifs to evoke the appropriate feeling.

Siegfried raises the drinking horn and takes a long draught. He returns the horn to Gutrune, who lowers her eyes in shame and confusion. Siegfried looks fixedly at her: his passion is quickly aflame. As if by lightning, he avers, she has affected him deeply. Why does she lower her eyes? Blushing, she raises them to his. After more expressions of his infatuation, he asks Gunther, in trembling voice, what is his sister's name. 'Gutrune', he answers. Then Siegfried softly asks whether he reads good omens in her eyes. He seizes her hand with impetuous ardour and asks her if she will refuse, as her brother did, to accept his devotion. She involuntarily catches Hagen's eye, bows her head submissively and, with a gesture of humility, leaves the hall with faltering steps. Siegfried gazes after her as if bewitched. Without turning to the other men, he asks Gunther if he has a wife. Not yet, replies the Gibichung, nor is he likely to find one easily, because the one on whom he has set his heart is on a rock protected by a fire. Siegfried has by now turned round and offered his help. Making a strenuous effort to retain a memory, he asks about the fire. Only that way, says Gunther, can someone be Brünnhilde's suitor. By now no memory of her shows in Siegfried's expression. Coming out of his reverie, he turns to Gunther and cheerfully offers to win him this woman. He is unafraid of the fire. In return he asks for Gutrune as his wife. He will trick Brünnhilde by use of the Tarnhelm's magic, disguising himself as Gunther. Siegfried then suggests an oath of blood-brotherhood to a new motif (61). Hagen fills a drinking horn with new wine, and holds it out for Siegfried and Gunther, who prick their arms with swords before holding them over the horn. Each lays two fingers on the horn, which is held between them by Hagen. Siegfried begins the oath, saying life was quickened by the freshening blood that he has poured in the draught. Gunther counters with a declaration of brotherly love. Then, together, they drink to loyalty, after which Siegfried holds out the empty drinking horn to Hagen who slices it in two with his sword. Gunther and Siegfried clasp hands. Siegfried looks at Hagen, who has been standing behind him during the oath-swearing, and asks why he has not joined in. He replies that his blood would poison the drink, for it is not pure and noble like theirs but, sluggish and cold, lies stagnant within him. So he holds aloof from fiery bonds. Gunther tells Siegfried to leave the surly man alone. The hero puts on his shield in preparation for the journey, and summons Gunther to his boat. Stepping closer to the Gibichung, he tells him that he must wait in the boat one night; then he will be able to bring home his wife. Siegfried, spurning rest, is ready to leave and unties the boat.

So the pair set out down the Rhine, Hagen having been asked by Gunther to guard the palace. While Siegfried and Gunther, having put their weapons in the boat, hoist the sail and prepare the craft, Hagen picks up his spear and shield. Gutrune appears just as Siegfried pushes out the boat immediately into midstream. She inquires whither they are hurrying. Sitting comfortably in front of the hall with his spear and shield, Hagen tells her that they have sailed to woo Brünnhilde because Siegfried is in such a hurry to have Gutrune as wife. With a cry of 'Siegfried – mine' she returns to her room excitedly. Siegfried has grasped the oar and now punts the boat downstream. It is soon lost to view.

Now comes the episode known as Hagen's Watch. As he sits motionless with his back against the door-post of the hall, he begins his sombre monologue in which he gloats over his coming triumph. Gunther wins himself a bride and Hagen the Ring. Gunther and Siegfried, sons of life, will soon be Hagen's vassals. Various of the Ring's darkest, most threatening themes make up the orchestral texture. Alberich's unseen presence seems to loom large. During the sombre orchestral interlude, the curtain in front of the hall is drawn. The music still tells us of Hagen's dark thoughts, but slowly, in another of Wagner's masterful transitions, the mood begins to change and more optimistic motifs, associated with Brünnhilde, suffuse the texture, although not without hints of Alberich's curse (17).

Scene 3

When the curtain is drawn for the third scene, the summit of
the rock is as it was in the Prologue, with Brünnhilde sitting at
the entrance to the cave. She is sunk in deep contemplation of
the Ring. Overwhelmed by happy memories, she covers it with
kisses. Distant thunder is heard; Brünnhilde looks up and
listens. Then she turns her attention once more to the Ring. A
flash of lightning comes and again she listens, peering into the
distance whence a dark thunder-cloud is approaching the
rock. She says that she can hear a familiar noise from the past.
A galloping horse is riding towards her. Who is seeking her out
in her solitude? It is Waltraute, who calls from afar, asking if
her sister is asleep or awake. Excitedly, Brünnhilde jumps up
from her seat, delighted by the thought of happy news (as she
imagines it to be). She calls to Waltraute (offstage), asking if it
is truly her sister, then hurries to the rock's edge and instructs
her to dismount in the wood, whither she herself now runs.
From there can be heard a clap of thunder. She returns elatedly
with Waltraute, not noticing her anxiety and fears.

Brünnhilde asks if her sister has been brave enough to come
to her. Waltraute replies that she has come solely for Brünnhilde's sake. Brünnhilde's first ecstatic thought is that Waltraute has come from Wotan with a message that his heart has
softened towards her – although she has not regretted her
punishment, since it has brought her a wonderful hero as
bridegroom. She embraces Waltraute with wild joy, which her
sister attempts to ward off, impatiently. But Brünnhilde continues in the same vein, asking if Waltraute has come to share
her delight. Waltraute vehemently cries that she has not come
to share in this foolish ecstasy, but for quite another reason.
Then Brünnhilde inquires if, in fact, Wotan has not pardoned
her after all. Has Waltraute come to her in fear of his rage?
Gloomily Waltraute replies that if that were all, her anguish
would be at an end, and she recounts in detail to the astonished
Brünnhilde the purpose of her visit.

Hers is a grand, tragic narration of the last assembling of the
gods in Valhalla. Since he parted from Brünnhilde, Wotan had

no longer sent the other Valkyries into battle; they have ridden aimlessly through the clouds in fear and trembling. Wotan himself roved solitarily and restlessly through the world. Once he came back to Valhalla with his spear splintered in his hand. Silently he motioned the heroes in Valhalla to cut down the tree from whose roots the spring of life and eternal wisdom flowed, and to pile up the wood round Valhalla's walls. This passage is solemnly accompanied by the Valhalla motif (7) and that of the god's distress (30). Then, calling the gods together, Wotan took his place among them. Now he sits there silent and motionless, clasping the pieces of the broken spear in his hand and not touching Holda's apples. Astonishment and fear have petrified the gods. Wotan has sent two ravens into the world. If they were to return to Valhalla with good news, the god would smile once again, for the last time in eternity. The Valkyries clasp his knees, and lie at his feet. Then, in one of the cycle's most moving passages, the weary god is reported as musing on his parting from Brünnhilde. With closed eyes, as if in a trance, he murmured the thought that if Brünnhilde were to give back the Ring to the Rhinemaidens, the gods and the world would be released from its terrible curse.

Having heard these words, Waltraute stole softly away from among the silent ranks and hastened to her sister's side. She entreats Brünnhilde to do the deed, and put an end to this universal misery. At this, she throws herself at Brünnhilde's feet. Tranquilly Brünnhilde replies that all this has no meaning for her. She has been separated for a long time from the cloudy heaven. To her Waltraute's eyes look tired, her cheeks wan. What is it that she must do? With anxious haste, Waltraute answers that she should fling the accursed Ring back to the Rhinemaidens. Brünnhilde counters that it is mad to expect that the Ring, pledge of Siegfried's love, could be given away. No amount of pleading from Waltraute will move her. She prizes the Ring more than all the joys of Valhalla, more than the eternal glory of the gods or their happiness. Not to save a world from destruction will she renounce love nor have the Ring taken from her. To these passionate declarations of

Brünnhilde's love the orchestra replies with the tragic motif of renunciation (6), for she will be compelled, by a force she cannot resist – by Siegfried himself – to give up the Ring to which she clings so resolutely; now, in the triumph of her love, she is blind to the curse and rushes to meet her doom.

Scene 4

Even as Waltraute, in despair, leaves her the flames once more begin to flicker round the rock. Brünnhilde commands the clouds and lightning not to return. It is evening and she looks out calmly at the view, declaring that the fire shines brightly round her. It seems to dart angrily up the summit.

Siegfried's horn call is now heard backstage. Brünnhilde listens and jumps up ecstatically, crying Siegfried's name. She runs to meet him in the utmost ecstasy. Flames arise and Siegfried jumps from them on to a high promontory. As he does, the fire recedes and flares only from the valley. Brünnhilde now shrinks back in fear, runs downstage from where she looks with speechless astonishment at Siegfried. He is disguised as Gunther, the Tarnhelm on his head covering the upper part of his face, only his eyes being visible. She cries that she has been betrayed and asks who has forced his way to her. As the motifs of deceit (58) and of the Gibichung (57) insinuate themselves into the orchestral tissue, Siegfried stands still on the rock at the back, leaning on his shield and observes Brünnhilde. Then, in a baritonal voice, he commands her to follow him, for she must be his wife. Trembling violently, she asks who is this intruder. Siegfried replies that he is a hero who will tame her. Seized with fear, she says that a demon has usurped the rock. She asks who is this terrible being, and after a long silence wants to know if he comes from Hella, host of night. At first in a trembling tone, then more forthrightly, Siegfried declares that he is Gunther, the hero to whom she will belong. She breaks out in despairing accents, blaming Wotan for this punishment, mockery and degradation. Siegfried jumps down from the rock and goes closer to her, saying that night is falling and that she must marry him in her abode. She tries to threaten him by holding up Siegfried's Ring and bidding him fear that symbol; it shall protect her from dishonour with its super-natural power. Siegfried counters that it must be given to Gunther as a husband's right. Brünnhilde orders the robber to stay his hand, but he will not be denied and hurls himself at her. After a violent struggle in which Brünnhilde several times breaks free, he wrests the Ring from her. She lets out a piercing cry and falls defeated into his arms. Her eyes unconsciously meet Siegfried's. He lets her fall limply on to the stone seat before her cave. All the while the most menacing motifs of the cycle rage against each other, in which that of Alberich's revenge (16) dominates. Siegfried declares that now she is his. Weak and exhausted, she asks how this wretched woman can defend herself. Siegfried pushes her toward the cave and she enters it with unsteady steps. Then Siegfried draws his sword and, in his natural voice, says that it shall separate him from his friend's bride. As the curtain falls he follows her into the cave.

ACT 2

Scene 1

The superb second act – Ernest Newman called it 'in some ways Wagner's supreme achievement in music drama' – finds the composer in absolute control of his motifs, subtly combin-ing them and weaving them in and out of the texture.

The prelude depicts the dark brooding of Alberich and his son Hagen. Evil deeds are obviously afoot. As the curtain rises, we see the shore in front of the Gibichung hall. Its open entrance is now on the right; on the left is the bank of the Rhine. Running across the back of the stage is a series of rocky heights, on which are erected various altar-stones, one to Fricka, one (higher up) to Wotan and another to Donner. It is night; Hagen is still asleep, leaning against one of the hall's columns with his spear on his arm, his shield by his side. The moon suddenly comes out and casts a harsh light on Hagen and his surroundings. Alberich comes into sight, crouching before Hagen and leaning his arms on Hagen's knees. Softly the dwarf asks his son if he is sleeping. In a trance-like state, yet with his eyes open, Hagen replies that he hears him. It is as if his evil *alter ego* were speaking to Hagen. They exchange thoughts on Hagen's mother, from whom Hagen is estranged. Alberich then recalls the supposed misdeeds of Wotan and describes his forthcoming fate. Hagen inquires who will inherit the treasure. Alberich insists it is they who will gain the world. Secretively he gloats over Siegfried's ignorance of the Ring's value; they must now destroy him – and that is precisely Hagen's intention. Alberich urges that Brünnhilde must not allow Siegfried to return the Ring to the Rhinemaidens. Now Hagen, man of hatred, must avenge Alberich, and destroy the Wälsung and Wotan. Does Hagen swear that?

Dawn begins to break. Hagen confirms that he will have the Ring and tells his father to stop worrying. During his final lines in the whole cycle (he is the only character to survive through all the operas), Alberich gradually disappears and his voice grows fainter as he calls repeatedly to Hagen to be faithful. Now he has quite vanished. Hagen, who has not moved throughout, stares with a glazed look at the Rhine over which the dawn's light is spreading.

Scene 2

As the second scene begins, the river starts to glow more and more brightly with the red light of dawn, but the warmth of the music is soured by hints of the Tarnhelm motif (12), as Hagen gives a start. Siegfried emerges suddenly from behind a tree on the river's bank. He is in his own form, but the Tarnhelm is still on his head. Taking it off and attaching it to his belt as he walks forward, he gives Hagen a cheerful greeting. The latter slowly rises to hear the news that Brünnhilde and Gunther are following more slowly by boat. Hagen calls into the palace for Gutrune so that he can tell her Siegfried is with them. Turning towards the hall, Siegfried tells them, as he answers Gutrune's eager questions, how he subdued Brünnhilde, and now comes to claim Gutrune as his wife. Her slight touch of jealousy at

Siegfried's having wooed Brünnhilde for Gunther is soon allayed – a sword had lain between Siegfried and Brünnhilde all night. Then, in the morning mist, Brünnhilde followed Siegfried to the valley, and when they were near the shore, Gunther swiftly took his place. Using the Tarnhelm, Siegfried had quickly transported himself back to the hall. Now the lovers are travelling up the Rhine. Gutrune happily hails Siegfried, as the strongest of men. Hagen, looking down from a promontory in the background, spots the sail, and joyfully Gutrune gives the bride a greeting, and bids Hagen and his vassals prepare for the wedding. As she walks towards the hall, she turns round and asks Siegfried if he needs rest. He replies that helping her is all the rest he requires. At that he takes her hand and they enter the hall.

Scene 3

Hagen now ascends a rock at the back of the stage, turns offstage and blows on his cow-horn. That uncouth, urgent sound begins the episode known as Hagen's Call, as he summons the vassals to assemble with their weapons for danger – indeed a crisis – is near. He remains at his post on the rock, and blows his horn again. Various cow-horns echo his call round the countryside, and a wild crew of armed men rush in from several quarters, first singly, then in groups. They gather on the shore in front of the hall.

There follows the first chorus heard in the whole *Ring*, to the accompaniment of the vassals' motif (62). They inquire why they have been summoned; Hagen, still on the promontory, replies that Gunther is returning with a bride. She will be alone, protected from harm by Siegfried, the dragon-killer. Sturdy steers must be slain so that Wotan's altar runs with their blood. A boar must be killed for Froh, a lusty goat for Donner, sheep for Fricka, so that she may look on the marriage with favour. The vassals, with growing amusement, ask what they must do after that. The reply comes that they must fill their drinking horns and let their wives prepare mead and wine, so that they can keep drinking until they collapse in a stupor. There is more merriment as they sing a boisterous song to this grim Hagen of theirs. The hawthorn, they declare, does not prick any more: he has become a herald of a wedding. Meanwhile Hagen has remained grave; now he comes down into the midst of the vassals, and tells them to stop laughing: they must prepare to greet Gunther's bride. He points down the Rhine, and they hurry, some to the top of the hill, some by the shore, to watch the arrival. Hagen goes up to some of the men and instructs them to be kind to their mistress, to serve her loyally and, if necessary, to be quick to avenge her. Now he goes slowly towards the back on one side. As the vassals sing their greetings, Gunther and Brünnhilde come into sight in their boat. The men who have been watching from the hill come down to the shore. Some now jump into the water and pull the boat to land. Finally, as the scene ends, they all crowd together closely along the bank.

Scene 4

The pair step out of their vessel. The vassals line up to give homage. Gunther ceremoniously leads Brünnhilde forward by the hand. In a massive chorus, the vassals give praise to the couple, clashing their weapons together and making a thunderous noise. As Gunther introduces Brünnhilde to the men, she follows him, her look pale and her eyes lowered. He presents her as his wife and a noble one. Now the Gibichungs will rise to a peak of fame. Solemnly beating their weapons, the men renew their praise. Gunther leads Brünnhilde, who still does not raise her eyes, towards the hall, from which Siegfried and Gutrune emerge, accompanied by her women. Gunther stops in front of the hall and greets the other pair and then declares that the two couples must celebrate together – Brünnhilde and Gunther, Gutrune and Siegfried. At this Brünnhilde raises her eyes in astonishment and, perceiving Siegfried, looks at him in amazement. She pulls her hand violently from Gunther's clasp, and he lets go of it, feeling as surprised as everyone else at her behaviour. The men and women wonder what is afoot, and Siegfried, taking a few steps towards

Brünnhilde, asks what disturbs her. Barely controlling herself, she can only cry 'Siegfried – here! Gutrune?' Siegfried replies that Gunther's gentle sister is married to him – as Brünnhilde is to Gunther. With terrible power, she exclaims that he is a liar, then staggers and appears to fall. Siegfried, who is nearest to her, supports her. Leaning wearily against him, she murmurs that he does not recognize her. He tells her to stand by her bridegroom. As she sees the Ring on Siegfried's outstretched hand, she exhorts Gunther in the greatest agitation to look at it. Something of the truth begins to dawn on her. Hagen, recognizing that the moment of decision has arrived, comes from the background and tells the men to harken to this woman's complaint. Attempting to pull herself together and restraining her violent excitement, Brünnhilde says to Siegfried that the Ring on his finger is not his but was wrested from her. Then, pointing to Gunther, she says that it was snatched by him. As he quietly contemplates the Ring, Siegfried says that he did not get it from Gunther. At this, Brünnhilde says to Gunther that he should demand back the Ring by which he had won her. Gunther is confused, but she demands to see the Ring stolen from her. The embarrassed Gibichung stays silent, at which Brünnhilde bursts out furiously that Siegfried is the deceitful thief. All eyes are now turned on Siegfried, who is lost in musing on the Ring. He declares that no woman gave him the Ring; he remembers well that it was the reward for his victory over a dragon.

Hagen now intervenes, telling the bewildered Brünnhilde that if she really recognizes the Ring, Siegfried won it through deceit, which he shall repent. Almost beside herself with sorrow and anger, Brünnhilde cries out frenziedly that she has been shamefully betrayed. Treachery such as this is beyond all vengeance. In a great outburst she now appeals to the gods, who have intended for her sorrow and shame such as has never been suffered before, to inspire her with such anger and vengeance as never raged before and to teach her to break her heart that she may ruin the man who has betrayed her. Gunther tries in vain to calm her. She cries out that she has been wedded, not to him but to Siegfried, adding sadly that he took love and happiness from her. The unknowing Siegfried in turn accuses her of being false and denies the charge of disloyalty to Gunther and Gutrune. Brünnhilde answers that it is Siegfried who is lying: that on the bridal night the sword had lain in its sheath against the wall while its owner made love to her. The men and women become violently indignant at this. Gunther and Gutrune now urge Siegfried to prove the falsity of Brünnhilde's accusations, while the men demand from him an oath that he is blameless.

At this crux of the drama, the vassals form a circle round Siegfried and Hagen. Hagen holds out his spear, on which the oath will be taken. Siegfried lays two fingers on its point, and solemnly swears that death shall take him if the woman spoke the truth (63): indeed, this spear will then strike him down – prophetic words. Bursting into the circle, Brünnhilde furiously pushes Siegfried's hand off the spear and places her own on its point. She swears that his oath is false and blesses the spear that it may avenge her wrongs. The excited vassals call on Donner to hurl down his thunder to silence this monstrous act. Siegfried tells Gunther to beware of his wife, because she has sworn this shameful lie. She must have some peace to calm this demon in her. Then he walks over to Gunther and tells him that the Tarnhelm must have only half disguised him. Still, angry women are soon calmed. Turning back to the vassals, he tells them to cheer up and follow him to the feast. He exhorts the women to enjoy the wedding. His natural high spirits now take hold of him, and in relaxed mood, he light-heartedly throws his arm round Gutrune and leads her into the hall. The men and women follow them. The stage is now empty except for Brünnhilde, Gunther and Hagen. The orchestra underlines feelings and the situation by the recollection of various motifs, now marvellously intertwined. Gunther, in deep shame and very perplexed, slumps down at one side of the stage, hiding his face in his hands. Hagen remains motionless behind Brünnhilde who stands downstage and gazes with pain after Siegfried and Gutrune for some time. Then she drops her head.

Scene 5

At last, engrossed in numbed thought, Brünnhilde begins the act's last scene by asking herself what evil craft lies hidden here, what magic has wrought such a terrible change in Siegfried. In her anguish she turns to the only means left to her of putting an end to it – revenge. But who will offer her a sword with which to sever the ties that still bind her to him? Now Hagen's moment has come, and stepping up to her, he tells her to trust him, and he will carry out her revenge. Looking round languidly, she asks, revenge on whom? 'On Siegfried', he replies. Brünnhilde laughs bitterly at Hagen's suggestion: a single glance of Siegfried's flashing eyes, which she knows so well, would put to flight all Hagen's valour. Even though the hero has sworn a false oath on Hagen's weapon, his victorious strength would protect him from all danger, for Brünnhilde has given Siegfried all the power she once possessed as Wotan's daughter, and with her magic has made him invulnerable. She cries out how ungrateful he has been and what a shameful reward she has received. Hagen then asks whether any weapon can harm Siegfried. She answers that he cannot be injured in battle, but she did not weave her spells on his back because he would never turn it on an enemy. Then, Hagen gleefully declares, it is there his spear will strike.

Turning swiftly to Gunther, he rouses him and tells him to stop brooding. Gunther passionately bewails the deceit that has been practised on him. Brünnhilde scornfully reproaches him with cowardice and treachery, saying that he hid himself behind Siegfried so that the latter might win her for him as a prize, and that the Gibichungs have indeed sunk low to produce such a faint-hearted creature. Her words drive Gunther to despair and, beside himself, he appeals to Hagen to redeem his honour. Hagen answers that nothing will help him except Siegfried's death. Gunther reminds him of the bond of brotherhood existing between them. Which he broke, Hagen interjects. Gunther asks if Siegfried really betrayed him. 'He did cheat you,' says Brünnhilde, and they have all cheated her, she adds. If she were to be avenged, all the blood in the world would not expiate their crime. But one death will suffice for all: Siegfried shall fall in atonement for himself and them. In an aside, Hagen tells Gunther that he will gain the enormous power of the Ring if Siegfried is killed. 'Brünnhilde's Ring?' asks Gunther quietly. 'The Nibelung's Ring,' exults Hagen. With a heavy sigh, Gunther says then it must be so, but concern for Gutrune makes him hesitate. At this, Brünnhilde furiously breaks out in realization that it is Gutrune who has bewitched Siegfried, enticed her husband away from her. Speaking to Gunther, Hagen says that Siegfried's death will make Gutrune sad, so the deed should be kept from her. Siegfried will be killed on the morrow while hunting; a boar will kill him. The three unanimously declare that it shall be so: Siegfried shall fall. Thus Brünnhilde and Gunther will be revenged for the wrong done them by the hero, and Hagen will achieve his object – to become master of the Ring. He exultantly invokes his father, Alberich while Brünnhilde calls upon Wotan to listen to their oath of vengeance. Their voices combine with Gunther's in an impressive trio, one of the cycle's few ensembles. As Gunther and Brünnhilde turn towards the hall, they encounter the wedding procession, with boys and girls waving flower-entwined branches. The men bear Siegfried on a shield and Gutrune on a chair. On the promontory at the back, vassals and maids bring sacrificial beasts to the altars. Siegfried and the vassals blow a wedding-call on their horns. The women invite Brünnhilde to join Gutrune, who beckons with a friendly smile. When Brünnhilde tries to draw back, Hagen quickly passes her over to Gunther, who takes her hand once more before he is raised high on a shield by the men. To a melding of motifs, Gutrune's predominating, before Hagen's strikes in, the procession moves towards the hill and the curtain falls.

ACT 3

Scene 1

The prelude begins with Siegfried's horn-call heard off-stage, answered by the cow-horns of the Gibichungs. Next we are reminded of the flowing Rhine by the familiar melodies of *Das Rheingold*. The curtain rises on a wild woodland, with the Rhine flowing past a steep cliff in the background. Woglinde, Wellgunde and Flosshilde rise to the surface of the water and swim about as if in a circling dance. The freshness and brightness of the scene remind us of the opening of the whole drama, when the beauty of nature was not clouded by the tragedy of human passion and sin. Nonetheless, the Rhinemaidens are well aware of what has happened. Together they say, in their sad songs, as they briefly stop swimming, that the Rhine's lustre no longer matches that of the sun, now that the gold has been stolen. (64). As they resume their swimming they sing their refrain. Now Siegfried's horn is heard in the distance, and their spirits revive as they splash about joyfully in the water. They plead to 'Lady Sun' to send them a hero who will give them back the gold.

Just before he enters, Siegfried's horn peals out above them. They cry out that their champion is near. As he appears on the cliff, they dive into the water. He is fully armed and wondering how he lost track of his fellow-hunters and his quarry. The Rhinemaidens rise to the surface again, (65) swimming in circles, and greet Siegfried. They tease him and exhort him to tell his tale. Smiling, he asks if they have lured away his prey – if so, they are welcome to the shaggy beast. Laughingly, they offer to give him what he is looking for in exchange for the Ring on his finger, but such an exchange does not seem to make sense to Siegfried. Only after a good deal of mocking laughter from the Rhinemaidens, and much diving and dancing on their part, does he offer the Ring. He takes it from his finger and holds it aloft. But now, when they reappear, they are in a more serious, even a solemn mood as they bid him keep it and learn what misfortune attaches to its possession. He calmly puts it back on his finger and asks them to say what they know.

Individually and in ensemble, they tell him its history: how it has been cursed by the man who first forged it, then lost it; as the appropriate motifs loom up in the orchestra, they warn

him of the fate awaiting him if he does not give the Ring back
to the Rhine. But if Siegfried was deaf to their mockery, he is
much more so to their threats, and he laughs at their warning.
As he looks at the Ring, he says that he won ownership of the
world through it but he would gladly give that up if he could
make love to them. He cares as little for his life as for the clod
of earth that he now picks up, holds above his head and then,
at the last words, throws behind him. The Maidens see that
their warning has no effect on the hero. In an excited state they
swim in wide circles close to the shore, singing that he has
thrown away a glorious possession (Brünnhilde's love) without knowing it, but will not give up the Ring that, if he keeps it,
condemns him to death. So, bidding him farewell, they swim
away singing, to warn Brünnhilde. From her they hope for a
better hearing. They resume their dance, then swim away to
the back, singing their song. Siegfried's smiling look follows
them; he sits on a rock by the bank with his head supported on
his hand, philosophizing that when women do not get their
way by flattery, they resort to threats, yet, if he was not true to
Gutrune he could have taken a fancy to one of the voluptuous
ladies.

He gazes after the Maidens without moving. They can be
heard from very far away.

Scene 2

Hunting horns are heard, growing closer all the time. Hagen is
heard calling from afar. Siegfried starts out of the reverie
which had taken him out of himself and replies to the call with
his own horn. He also gives an answering call with his voice;
this produces, in turn, a response from the vassals. Hagen
appears on the cliff with Gunther folllowing him. Siegfried
invites them down to where it is fresh and cool. The vassals
having now arrived they all move down to join Siegfried.
Hagen says they will rest there and have a meal. The game is
piled in a heap, wineskins and drinking-horns are produced,
and all lie down. Hagen asks Siegfried how he has fared in his
hunting. He answers that he is ill-provided for the meal; he has

found only water-fowl, three wild water birds, who said he would be murdered that day. He lies down between Gunther and Hagen. Gunther shudders and looks gloomily at Hagen, who remains unmoved, saying that it would be a poor hunt if the unsuccessful hunter were killed by a lurking beast. Now Siegfried complains of thirst, and a drinking-horn is filled, which Hagen hands to him, asking if it is really true that he understands bird-song. Siegfried answers that it is a long time since he paid heed to their chatter. Then he takes the drinking-horn and turns to Gunther, offering the horn to him as his brother. Gunther looks gloomily and broodingly into the horn before muttering that the draught is flat and pale; Siegfried's blood alone is in it. Laughing, Siegfried says that he will mix it with Gunther's, and pours Gunther's drink into his own horn so that it overflows; Mother Earth has made it flow over, he declares joyfully, but Gunther sighs at his friend's vivacity. Siegfried asks Hagen quietly if Brünnhilde is still bothering Gunther. Hagen replies that it is a pity that he does not understand her as well as Siegfried does bird-song. Turning joyously to Gunther, Siegfried says he will cheer him up with stories of his youth. Gunther replies that he would like to hear them.

Everyone now lies round Siegfried while he sits upright. As the appropriate motifs are recalled, he recounts his education at Mime's hands, how he forged the sword, slew the dragon, learnt how to understand the birds from the taste of the dragon's blood, had then taken the Tarnhelm and Ring from the cave, and killed the treacherous dwarf. As he relates the last exploit, Hagen's demoniacal laughter reminds us of the mirth with which Alberich had witnessed his brother's fate. Now, before the story continues, Hagen drops the juice of a herb into Siegfried's horn and we hear an echo of the music that accompanied his drinking the draught of oblivion. Hagen then offers the horn to Siegfried to help him refresh his memory. The hero looks thoughtfully into the horn, drinks slowly, and goes on with his story. He now tells of the Woodbird's good advice, as Gunther listens with growing amazement, he describes his ascent to the mountain through the fire, while the orchestra recalls the inspiriting motifs of *Siegfried*, Act 3. As his ecstasy grows, Siegfried relates how he found and awakened Brünnhilde. Gunther now jumps up, deeply shocked and exclaims: 'What do I hear?' The motif of the curse (17) resounds as two ravens fly up from a bush, circle over Siegfried's head and go off towards the Rhine. Hagen asks if he can understand what the ravens are saying. Siegfried jumps up and looks for them. He turns his back on Hagen as he looks towards the ravens. Hagen plunges his spear into Siegfried's back, declaring that, to him, the birds cry revenge. Too late Gunther strikes Hagen's arm. Siegfried lifts up his shield with both hands and attempts to crush Hagen, but his strength fails him; his shield drops behind him, and he falls on to it with a crash. Four vassals try vainly to restrain Hagen, asking him first what he is doing, and then what he has actually done. Pointing to the prostrate body, he declares that he has avenged perjury. He turns quietly, and disappears over the brow of hill. He is seen moving away slowly through the dusk that had begun to fall when the ravens appeared. Gunther, grief-stricken, bends over Siegfried. The vassals stand sympathetically round the dying man.

Helped by two vassals, Siegfried sits up and opens his eyes uttering, in a radiant voice, Brünnhilde's name, calling her holy bride. The present and near past have faded from his memory. In spirit, he is again bending over the the form of the sleeping Valkyrie and we hear the music of her awakening, with its delicate harp accompaninent. He recalls every episode of that happy occasion, now made almost unbearably poignant. In the light of those eyes, now eternally open for him, with the air fanning his cheek, like the warm breath from her lips, he feels once more the ecstasy of love. He once more calls her name, then sinks lifeless to the ground. A moment of solemn silence ensues. The men round Siegfried are sorrowful, but stay still. Night has fallen. At a silent command from Gunther the vassals lift Siegfried's body on to his shield and slowly carry it in solemn procession over the rocks. Gunther follows behind the corpse.

There follows the grand, sorrowing Funeral March, the cycle's most noble moment. Various motifs characterizing the hero are transmuted into tragic grandeur as the sufferings of the Wälsung race are adumbrated and its last scion has worked out his own destiny, before finally returning in spirit to his pure love. As the mourning procession passes from sight, the moon breaks through the clouds and illuminates the funeral procession more and more brightly as it reaches the summit of the cliff. Mists rise from the Rhine and gradually wrap the scene in darkness, Eventually the stage is completely veiled. When the mists are dispelled, we are back in the Gibichung's Hall, as in Act 1.

Scene 3

The third and final scene of the Act begins in the darkness of night, with the moonlight reflected on the Rhine. Gutrune comes out of her room into the hall. She watches and listens anxiously for Siegfried's return. We hear his motif (39) resound in a sad minor key. Nightmares have disturbed her. She has seen a woman's form glide to the water's edge. Was it Brünnhilde, whom she dreads? She listens at the door on the right and calls to Brünnhilde. Opening the door timidly, she looks into the inner room, but finds the apartment empty. She is frightened, and hears a distant call. Was it Siegfried's horn? No; ominous silence reigns over all. She turns to go back to her own room, but hearing Hagen's voice, she pauses, petrified by fear.

Hagen's voice, accompanied by motifs referring to his treachery and Alberich's revenge, is heard off-stage, hailing the household with coarse calls. He bids everyone awaken and bring torches, for he brings back the spoils of the hunt. Light and growing fires are seen outside as Hagen comes into the hall. He tells Gutrune to arise and welcome Siegfried, the strong champion returning home. In great anxiety, she asks what has happened, as she has not heard her champion's horn. A crowd of men and women enter with lights and flaming torches, joining the procession of the vassals carrying Siegfried's body; among them is Gunther. Hagen declares that the hero will blow his horn no more, nor pay court to beautiful women. With mounting horror, Gutrune asks what they are bringing. The procession halts in the middle of the hall, and the soldiers put down the body on a hastily erected dais. Hagen says that Siegfried has been slain by a wild boar. Crying out, Gutrune collapses on top of the corpse. The distracted crowd is shocked and begins to lament. Gunther tries to comfort his sister, and begs her to open her eyes. Recovering consciousness, she pushes Gunther violently away, accusing him of murdering her husband. He replies that it is not he but Hagen: he is the cursed boar who has murdered that noble man. Defiantly Hagen steps forward, indifferent to Gutrune's sorrow and Gunther's angry repoaches. Indeed, he exalts in his deed and claims the Ring as reward. He is about to seize it when Gunther intervenes, claiming the Ring as Gutrune's legacy. Drawing his sword, Hagen declares that it is the dwarf's legacy, and attacks Gunther, who defends himself. A fight ensues. In vain the vassals try to intervene. Gunther falls dead from one of Hagen's blows. Now Hagen steps forward to seize the prize from Siegfried's hand, but the dead hand raises itself menacingly. Gutrune and the women shriek with horror. Everyone stands riveted to the spot in terror and amazement.

As the clamour subsides, Brünnhilde enters from the back, slowly and solemnly. While still at the rear she bids everyone to cease their wailing then walking forward, she adds that she would liken it to that of children whining to their mothers: she has not heard a lament befitting the hero. Getting up from the floor violently, Gutrune reproaches Brünnhilde for bringing this tragedy on them all. Brünnhilde waves her aside, saying that she was Siegfried's true wife, long before he set eyes on Gutrune, who was only his mistress. Gutrune now recognizes this to be the truth, that only through Hagen's magic drug had she been able to bind Siegfried to her, and she bitterly curses Hagen as the cause of all her misery. Then, leaving Siegfried's body, she falls on that of her brother, giving rein to all her sorrows, and stays motionless until the end. Hagen, remaining defiantly apart from the others and leaning on his spear, is sunk in thought at the opposite side.

Alone, at stage centre, Brünnhilde stands for a long time, shocked. Then, with solmen exaltation, she bids the vassals build a funeral pyre on the banks of the Rhine. She and her horse will be burnt with Siegfried. During the following, the younger vassals erect a large pyre in front of the hall beside the Rhine. The women adorn it with rugs on which they strew herbs and flowers. Brünnhilde is once more lost in thought as she contemplates the face of the dead man. Gradually her own face is transfigured with tenderness as she begins her final, noble utterance.

He was, she says, like the purest sunlight. He betrayed her, yet he was true. Indeed, a truer man than he never took an oath, a more honest man never fell in love. How could it happen that such a man could be a traitor? Looking up, she answers herself: it was the gods, Wotan foremost among them, who brought this woe on them. She asks them to look down on her sorrow, recognizing that Siegfried's bravest deed, so desired by Wotan – the acquisition of the Ring – was the cause of the hero's ruin. She sees, too, that only through the sorrow occasioned by his treachery has she herself regained the wisdom that she had renounced so willingly for human love. Now the same love, purified from all that is sensual and selfish, has become a divine love, an intense sympathy for human suffering. The ravens are meanwhile flapping their wings. They are sent by Brünnhilde home to Valhalla. With pity in her heart she murmurs to Wotan to rest himself.

At a sign from her, the vassals lift Siegfried's body on to the pyre. At the same time Brünnhilde removes the Ring from Siegfried's finger and gazes at it. Now she will take again her legacy, the accursed, terrible Ring. Addressing the Rhinemaidens, she tells them they will have back their gold, which they so much desire. The fire that consumes her body will cleanse the Ring from the curse and out of her ashes they will receive back their gold. In the water they will purify it, this bright gold stolen so horribly from them. Now Brünnhilde puts on the Ring, turns to the pyre, and snatches a huge fire brand from one of the vassals. Once more she commands the ravens to fly home. They must tell their master what they have heard by the Rhine. They shall travel past Brünnhilde's rock where Loge's fire is blazing. They must order Loge back to Valhalla for the end of the gods is nigh. She then declares that she will throw the torch at Valhalla's glittering castle.

Brünnhilde hurls the torch on to the pile of logs, which swiftly burst into flame. The two ravens fly up from the rock on the shore and disappear into the background. Two of the vassals lead in Brünnhilde's horse, which she greets from a distance. Then she runs towards Grane and unbridles him. She talks to him in loving, intimate terms. Does he know where she is taking him? At this point we hear the motif of love's redemption (34). Motif follows motif as she tells the beast that in the fire he will meet his master. Does he not want to join Siegfried, drawn by the flames? In her breast a bright fire also burns. In an ecstasy she longs to enfold Siegfried, to be embraced by him, in unending love to be united with him. Recalling her Valkyrie cry she shouts out Siegfried's name, and jumps on her horse and, spurring on Grane, leaps into the flames. Immediately they flare more fiercely so that the fire fills the whole of the area in front of the palace and appears to engulf it as well. The horrified vassals and women draw back to the front of the stage. Just when the whole stage seems to be filled with flames, the glow dies down, leaving behind only a cloud of smoke. This drifts towards the background, where it lies on the horizon as black cloud-bank. At the same time the Rhine overflows its banks and rolls in flood over the embers. Above the pyre the Rhinemaidens appear on a wave. Hagen, who, since the episode with Ring, has never taken his gaze from Brünnhilde, and has watched her with growing anxiety, is filled with terror when he sees the Rhinemaidens. Hastily throwing aside his spear, shield and helmet, he plunges headlong into the water crying 'Get away from the Ring.' Woglinde and Wellgunde throw their arms round his neck and drag him, as they swim backwards, into the depths, while Flosshilde, leading her sisters, exultantly holds aloft the recovered Ring. Their song is heard in the orchestra followed by the Valhalla motif (7), as a red glow penetrates the cloud-bank at the rear. As it grows, the Rhinemaidens are seen happily disporting themselves with the Ring and swimming in the now calm waves of the Rhine, which is gradually falling to its normal level. From the ruins of the hall, the vassals and women watch with disbelief as fire spreads over the sky. When it finally attains its full brightness, the main room of the castle of Valhalla is seen: assembled in it are the gods and heroes, just as Waltraute described them in the first Act. As the motif of the gods' downfall (18) thunders out, flames seize Valhalla. The gods are hidden from view by the conflagration as the curtain falls. As if to signify this ultimate cleansing, the final word is given to the theme representing the redemption of love (34). There is, at the last, a sense of sublimity and peace.

If, as Wagner himself wrote, 'The art of composition is the art of transition', then he was never truer to his own word than in *Götterdämmerung*, where the change from one scene to the next is handled in a masterly, unfaltering manner and with a perfect sense of timing. At the same time, the climax of the whole *Ring* cycle shows Wagner at zenith of his powers in another respect: the handling of his motifs. Where, in the earlier works, some of these appear too obviously or for no very good reason, in the tetralogy's finale they are woven inextricably and subtly into the texture of the music with an unerring sense of their musical and psychological purpose. This mastery is achieved over the widest span of music even Wagner had, as yet, attempted, the first act alone running to about two hours. During the course of that time, Wagner has presented us with a panorama of love and betrayal, good and evil, subconscious and overt events, grand, pictorial and private, intimate scenes. For each, he has found precisely the right musical colour, the most apt expression of words and mood. The earlier operas, as I have said, each have their own particular texture. In a sense, *Götterdämmerung* encompasses them all, puts all the strands heard before into a new perspective as the final tragedy approaches.

The second act, which has been called too 'operatic' in the bad old sense, is, on the contrary, a marvellous raising of the old convention to a higher purpose. Even the trio which ends the act, one of the *Ring*'s very few ensembles, is like no other trio heard before, serving the purpose of showing us how three minds have come together, for very different reason, to engineer Siegfried's downfall. In this act, we also have the cycle's only chorus, and just because we have not heard one before, its effect, quite apart from musical rightness of the vassals' offering, is arresting. Hereabouts, as nowhere else in the whole work, the real world seems briefly to impinge upon the mythical one, exerting a powerful contrast with what has gone before, what is to come.

In the final act, after Siegfried's brief interlude with the Rhinemaidens – an interlude that, just at the right moment, gives some release from the tension and dark deeds that precede and follow it – Wagner summons up all his powers to give us the unforgettable end to the great drama. Siegfried's recollection of his past, his death scene, the Funeral March and, finally, the Immolation are at the summit of Wagner's achievement as dramatist and composer. They defy description and, in an appropriate performance, leave the audience moved beyond measure. The challenge of this endlessly engrossing work has again been met, and the transfiguring power of love and its musical expression have overcome the work's seeming paradoxes.

Those paradoxes, as Andrew Porter has indicated,* concern the divided counsels of Wotan's Will, the often unheroic action of the hero Siegfried, prey to magic potions, Brünnhilde's often all-too-human passions. Yet all is put right in the end by the transfiguring power of love, which can wash away not only the posturings of Valhalla and the greed of the Nibelungs but also the sometime erring souls of Brünnhilde

---

* *About the House* Volume 5 No. 6. Summer 1978.

and Siegfried. And in *Götterdämmerung*, perhaps more than in any other of Wagner's works – certainly more than in *The Ring* as a whole – we have peered into our own souls, to our inner psyche, to try to discover a meaning for ourselves. That each generation comes away from the cycle with a different explanation, finds fresh revelations in the words and music, is the essence of its continuing worth and compelling power. Everyone should experience that power at least once in their lifetime – but then once is hardly likely to prove enough.

Appendix 1
Music Examples

Wagner's Ring

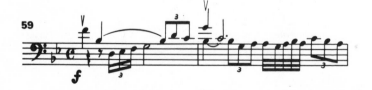

Appendix 2
Complete Performances on Record

Who would have guessed in 1958, when Decca with much trepidation began its recording of a complete cycle with *Das Rheingold* that by now there would have been eight versions of the cycle, even more if you include the briefly available 1953 Keilberth and 1968 Swarowsky sets. Of course, three of the performances (the two Furtwänglers, and the Knappertsbusch) predate the Solti, but they have only been issued to the general public in recent years.

There is a marked division on these complete sets between those that are a record, in the strictest sense of the word, of performances in the opera house and in one case, Furtwängler's Rome version, of a concert *Ring* for the radio, and those made in the studio. Nobody has put the advantages of live recordings more succinctly and accurately than that eminent Wagnerian, the late Deryck Cooke, writing in *Gramophone*: 'It means that we have a spontaneous, living, public performance from beginning to end, instead of a skilful amalgamation of the best bits of several attempts, a passage at a time, made in the laboratory of the recording studio'. I should add, in fairness to Mr Cooke's memory, that he did not overlook the disadvantages of recording in the theatre – mainly the inability to correct mistakes that may become tiresome on repetition – but in the cases under consideration here, they dwindle into insignificance before the greater reality. It is noteworthy that it is in the Wagnerian field, far more than any other, that live recordings have been favoured. There are three reasons for that phenomenon. Bayreuth is an excellent opera house in which to make records and its performances have a unique aura about them; Furtwängler and Knappertsbusch (probably the two greatest Wagner interpreters of the past fifty years) worked far more successfully in the theatre than out of it; and in the 1970s – another unique occurrence – the English-language, Goodall *Ring* at the Coliseum – was recorded at various performances for posterity through the generosity of the Peter Moores Foundation.

That recording was spread over five years, but it still has a unity about it not achieved in the Solti set (*S*), which was also recorded over a longish period (eight years) during which Solti seemed to alter his view considerably. I propose to discuss these studio sets before turning to those recorded live (I do not intend to waste space on the Swarowsky account, inferior in almost every respect).

As Wolfram Schwinger, the German critic has commented, Karajan's reading (*K*) 'fascinates by virtue of its radiant clarity, its virtuosity of sound, its highly effective contrasts, its *cantabile* quality, and its noble vocal and instrumental beauty', in comparison with the 'ecstatic dynamism' of (*S*). Both performances were made specifically with the gramophone in mind (although Karajan uses casts that had been assembled for performances at the Salzburg Easter Festival). Karajan uses the resources of the studio, as always, to entrance the ear and fascinate the mind with sensuous sound, bringing forward detail too often lost in the theatre. In *Rheingold* and *Götterdämmerung*, the most successful performances, the requisite Wagnerian energy and epic quality are also there; in the two middle operas, Karajan's chamber-music approach sometimes detracts from the sweep and strength of Wagner's vision, and the sheerly beautiful sound is often bought at the expense of the elemental force that must and does pervade the greatest interpretations. Still, as in *Siegfried*, when the hero reaches the mountain-top and awakes Brünnhilde, the glory of Karajan's unrivalled Berlin Philharmonic is almost seductive enough to set aside other considerations.

Solti never neglects the work's grander aspects, and throughout the cycle he makes the *Ring* exciting as a story. Aided by that more-than-lifelike recording technique of John Culshaw's team, with stage details made manifest in the home and movement to match, this is undoubtedly an exciting experience in the home. It is surely the set by which a whole generation of Wagner-lovers will have got to know the work. Those who have enjoyed it – and the immediate thrills are apparent enough – may wonder why other conductors in the theatre or on record approach the vast work with less emphasis on the excitements of the moment or why in other sets the orchestra plays less potently. In other words, Solti and Decca between them have realized the cycle brilliantly on one plane, but others are left unexposed. This is, as Decca once called it, 'Sonicstage' *par excellence*.

Solti's other merit lies in his cast, in spite of the changes which were for one reason or another needed during the course of the cycle's recording (incidentally it was not recorded in sequence, as a glance at the discography will show). Karajan's singers were carefully chosen, but they are on the whole less consistent in approach. In *Rheingold*, Solti's team has a definitely veteran feeling about it, except for George London's youthful-sounding Wotan. Set Svanholm's straightforward Loge and Kirsten Flagstad's staid but grandly sung Fricka have by now something of a historic importance to them. Gustav Neidlinger as Alberich is at the height of his powers for Solti: a menacing, confident performance that has set standards not yet equalled, let alone surpassed. He fulfils the view of Alberich as Wotan's alter ego better than any. Karajan has an exaggerated but brilliant Loge in Gerhard Stolze, a good second to Neidlinger in Zoltan Kelemen as Alberich, a Wotan in Fischer-Dieskau who matches his conductor in intelligence and subtlety but lacks vocal heft, a characterful Fricka in Josephine Veasey, the best of Fasolts in Martti Talvela (so moving in his farewell to Freia) and a winning, firm trio of Rhinemaidens.

In *Walküre*, Solti again fields a much more experienced team than Karajan, and this time it is an undoubted advantage. Régine Crespin's Brünnhilde (*K*) has marvellous moments – 'Zu lieben was du liebst' is just one, so heartfelt – but she is no match for Birgit Nilsson (*S*), who encompasses the character's expression of sympathy, grief, passion and finally humility – not with ideal individuality or warmth but with unfailing response to Wagner's vocal demands. Her Wotan is the incomparable Hans Hotter, no more, in his late fifties, the Titan he was for Knappertsbusch (see below) but still showing an unrivalled authority and subtlety. To passage after passge he brings a Lieder-singer's attention to meaning and detail. The depth of the god's anguish, misery, bitterness, love is expressed throughout this great portrayal, a command that Thomas Stewart (*K*), for all his intelligence, cannot match. Christa Ludwig (*S*) is an admirable Fricka and with Hotter the Wotan-Fricka scene goes magnificently – 'Deine ew'gen Gatlin' rolls off her tongue in dignified fashion – but she does not, in this part, sing with the assurance of Veasey (*K*).

For Solti, Crespin has reverted to Sieglinde, not as personal in expression as some and too careful in the love duet but rising finely to 'O hehrstes Wunder'. She is partnered by James King, virile of voice, pedestrian in interpretation. Jon Vickers as Siegmund (*K*) is as intense and committed as one might expect but also too artificial in some of his effects. Gundula Janowitz, his Sieglinde, is unexpectedly rapturous, nowhere more so than in the phrases 'Doch nein! Ich hörte sie neulich'. Karajan's reading, for all its restraint, has many moments such as these of vocal revelation. No wonder singers adore him so. Gottlob Frick's Hunding (*S*) is dark and dour, Talvela's (*K*) hardly less so.

The Solti *Siegfried* is again more obviously histrionic, big-scaled. In the title role, Wolfgang Windgassen, as we know now a late replacement for Ernst Kozub, gives one of the performances of his life; his tone may tend to dryness, but his deeply felt, thoughtful assumption showing disgust with Mime, impetuosity when sword-forging, eloquence in the forest, loneliness (wonderful passage) after killing Mime and in 'Selige Öde' are nowhere matched by Jess Thomas (*K*); for all his clear enunciation and clean tone, his singing is anything but heroic. In the final scene he is no match for Helga Dernesch's radiant Brünnhilde. At 'wild wütende Weib' she sounds just like that. 'Ewig war ich' is intimate and sensitive. Nilsson (*S*) is just as impressive, taking 'Heil dir, Sonne' in one breath in goddess-like voice, and melting into womanly vulnerability at 'Dort seh ' ich Grane'.

Hotter (*S*) wobbles in Act 1, but a single phrase 'und dass doch das liebeste ihm lebt?', so expressive, so authoritative, makes one forgive the apparent vocal decline. Stewart does not equal him here, or in the world-weariness of his final appearance. Stolze's more natural, less exaggerated Mime (*K*) is much preferable to his other, cackling self (*S*). There is not much to choose between the adequate but, Neidlinger's Alberich apart, not extraordinary interpreters of the smaller parts.

In *Götterdämmerung*, Dernesch as Brünnhilde (*K*) – obviously overstretched by the role but often singing with noble beauty – is surpassed by Nilsson, but for all her heroic stature there is more in the role than she finds. Windgassen (*S*) is again to be appreciated but here he is not a match for his younger self in other sets. Helge Brilioth (*K*) is a scrupulous musician with the right voice but only in Act 3 do his interpretative gifts show themselves. As Waltraute, Ludwig is too much the tragedy queen in both sets, but especially for Solti. The vocal competence is never in question. Frick's assurance as Hagen (*S*) is vitiated only by melodramatic touches, but he certainly chills the marrow more than the almost world-weary Karl Ridderbusch (*K*). Fischer-Dieskau's Gunther (*S*) would surely have outwitted the most wily gnome's son. More conventional vacillation and craven weakness is to be heard from Stewart (*K*). Claire Watson is a febrile Gutrune (*S*), Janowitz too cool. Adequate Norns in both sets, superb Rhinemaidens in Karajan's.

Before considering the most searching albeit very different

interpretations, I will deal with the Karl Böhm/Bayreuth performance, not to dismiss it but to place it perhaps one or two rungs lower than those discussed below. It must be listened to, 'viewed' is perhaps the *mot juste*, in relation to the Wieland Wagner production of the time, his second attempt at staging the great work of his grandfather. With the help of the copious illustrations in the accompanying booklet in its most recent manifestation, it is possible to transport oneself back to Bayreuth, 1966–7, when the recordings were made.

Böhm's interpretation, as can be confirmed in the 1969 Bayreuth listings of various conductors' times, is on the fast side (though not as fast as Boulez more recently). That can come as a relief after too many slow performances (for example Goodall's), and the quicker tempi, particularly in the context of a live recording, make for a more direct, dramatic reading. Certain passages that can seem portentous, even dull, in the wrong hands at a slower pace, are gathered together here into the sweep of a convincing interpretation – the 'colourful, pulsating, *al fresco* style', as Schwinger put it. Wotan's Narration in *Walküre*, the opening of *Siegfried*, Act 2, the end of that act, the Norns' and transformation scenes in *Götterdämmerung* are instances of his dynamic approach, while the surge of the *Walküre* love music or the different ardour of the *Siegfried* finale find in Böhm an admirably inspiring conductor.

By and large he is extraordinarily faithful to the composer's markings. So often other conductors ignore Wagner's injunction for movement, 'sehr belebt', or else make a *rallentando* before it is required. Böhm is always scrupulous in their observation. If all that suggests something of the *Kappellmeister* approach, it would be right. In certain grave passages, as the introduction to the *Todesverkündigung*, where rests are liberally asked for by Wagner, Böhm ignores them, and at his pace the Funeral March is not the noble tragedy it should be. Still, the interpretation is, on the whole, valid in its own right and an often welcome antidote to more ponderous ones. The Bayreuth orchestra, here a wonderful instrument, finds an honest, natural relationship with the singers not evident, or sought, on the studio-made sets.

Böhm's cast is not uniformly excellent, but Nilsson's tireless Brünnhilde, not surprisingly more involved than for Solti and showing a keen understanding of the character's development, together with Windgassen's Siegfried, unfailingly musical and miraculously fresh, except at the end of *Siegfried*, are the summation of these two artists' Wagnerian work (their Bayreuth *Tristan* excepted). James King's Siegmund, heard to greater advantage than for Solti, is possibly his best performance in any part on record: he benefits greatly from Böhm's speeds. So does Theo Adam as Wotan, taking many passages in a single breath that Wagner surely intended to be sung that way but which become impossible to mange thus at a slower pace. Adam's interpretation is at times prosaic, not sufficiently inward or anguished, yet he is a straightforward singer in sympathy with Böhm's approach.

Several other Bayreuth stalwarts of the 1960s are represented here. Leonie Rysanek, not in best voice, is still an appreciable Sieglinde, expressive and, above the stave, thrillingly intense. Neidlinger's Alberich is as strongly sung and characterized as ever. The three veteran basses, Kurt Böhme (a sinister, lugubrious Dragon), Josef Greindl (though now hard-pressed as Hagen), and Gerd Nienstedt are a formidable trio in their various incarnations. The young Talvela is a moving Fasolt once again.

Rheingold is weakened by Windgassen's underplayed Loge, but has Erwin Wohlfahrt's exemplary Mime, also an asset in *Siegfried*. The weaker ladies of the cycle are well represented by Anja Silja and Ludmila Dvorakova. Vera Soukupová's fruity Erda, Anneliese Burnmeister's blustery Fricka are less admirable, Martha Mödl, once a great Brünnhilde (see below), gives a Waltraute full of vocal insights but requires indulgence for tonal unevenness. Among the Valkyries, nobody could miss the potential (later fulfilled) of Dernesch or Danica Mastilovic but others sound overdue for retirement from hunting duties.

The Knappertsbusch *Ring* of a decade earlier, at last available, is at the opposite end of interpretation from Böhm, grand and conceptual where Böhm's is lyrical and impulsive. To me it is a magisterial and central achievement, delivered in long, lucid paragraphs, a feeling not always evident in encountering individual episodes. Although by Bayreuth timings, Knappertsbusch's are slow, they are considerably faster than Goodall's, because Knappertsbusch, unlike his English disciple, knew just when not to dally. Then passages such as Siegfried's Rhine Journey have a joyous energy not found in the English conductor's reading. Knappertsbusch also knew better than any how to conjure up a sonorous glow from Bayreuth acoustic. That, and so much else, makes his reading a deeply spirital journey almost on a par with his *Parsifal*. Knappertsbusch eschews obvious beauty of detail or momentary revelations, but I believe that what is sacrificed in that respect is amply compensated for by the profundity of the whole.

The singers are those most closely associated with Bayreuth in the 1950s, one of its greatest eras. The cast is headed by Hotter's again authoritative, introspective Wotan, offering unforgettable and influential insights not equalled by his often imitative successors. At times, during the first part of *Walküre*, Act 3, and in the Siegfried colloquy with Erda, the voice becomes unsteady and 'woofy' in that peculiarly Hotter manner, but for the rest the reading has potent inevitability of utterance. Here Hotter is caught in his prime for future generations to wonder at (I hope). Nowhere is that more so than in the dialogue with Fricka, the movingly sustained monologue and, of course, in the tender, paternal farewell. In *Rheingold* and in the second act of *Siegfried*, his encounters with Neidlinger's Alberich, here at the peak of his vocal powers, are the epitome of intelligent Wagnerian interpretation, subtly supported by the conductor.

Varnay's interesting Brünnhilde is also here preserved as a whole for posterity. The vocal mechanism is, as always with this singer, not faultless, but the sense of a total being involved is matched only by her contemporary, Mödl, for Furtwängler, and her singing is not technically at ease either. Perhaps a lack of perfection in tonal production induces greater thought about verbal meaning. Listen to how Varnay unforgettably inflects 'Siegfried kennt mich nicht' in Act 2 of *Götterdäm-merung*, the phrase and enunciation compounded of distress, anger and shock, or the incredulity of 'bist du von Sinnen?' in the conversation with sister Waltraute. The finale of *Siegfried*, though impressive, does not have Nilsson's gleam. Nilsson herself is here engaged as Sieglinde, eager, youthful but not ideally warm. Almost needless to say, she is magnificent in 'O hehrstes Wunder'. Her Siegmund is the highly intelligent Ramon Vinay, not very lyrical, but intense and articulate in declamatory passages.

In *Rheingold*, we meet the veteran Ludwig Suthaus (success-ively Siegmund and Siegfried for Furtwängler – see below) as a musically free, occasionally unsteady and consistently vivid Loge, Paul Kuen as a keen-edged, occasionally exaggerating Mime (still more detailed in *Siegfried*), Elisabeth Grümmer's ideally life-giving Freia, Josef Traxel's beautifully sung Froh, Arnold van Mill's lucid, eloquent Fasolt. Greindl, here as Fafner, even more as Hunding and Hagen, uses his dark-hued, sinister bass to telling effect. Georgine von Milinkovic is a conventional Fricka. Maria von Ilosvay (Covent Garden's Fricka in the 1950s) is a moderate Erda, an unaffected, urgent Waltraute. She is also a grave Norn; so is Nilsson – casting from strength indeed. Hermann Uhde's Gunther is an unsur-passed study of weakness, sung in that paradoxically com-manding way of his.

What of the hero? Bernd Aldenhoff, then near the end of his career, stepped in at short notice (for an indisposed Windgas-sen) for Siegfried. He still produces authentic *Heldentenor* sounds, and suggests more intelligence than he was given credit for. Some intrusive vibrato and the occasional inaccu-rate bray can be excused in a portrayal that produces the youthful brashness of the character, but he displays little of the poetry of Windgassen, who returns for *Götterdämmerung* to display his freshest singing in any cycle. One oddity: Knappertsbusch cuts the first verse of the second forging song in the *Siegfried*.

Furtwängler must wait in the wings no longer. Legends when closely investigated do not always live up to their reputation: not so with Furtwängler's performance of the *Ring* at La Scala in March and April 1950. It is emphatically not for the hi-fi enthusiast, nor even for those who may just about accept Knappertsbusch's very adequate mono sound, nor for those who require technical perfection in musical matters. Here we are offered an unvarnished look at the truth. There are audience coughs to contend with (the Italians sometimes seem unforgivably inattentive to the aural feast laid out before them), tape joins are abrupt, recorded levels alter, prompts are audible, side changes are rudely done, entries are sometimes muffed. If you can overcome and forget these human and mechanical flaws, you will be rewarded by a reading of lifetime from a great conductor at the peak of his power. The perfectly adequate Rome concert hall performance is surpassed in almost every way by this incandescent account, which holds one in thrall right from the announcement of the gold motif in the opening scene of *Rheingold* through to the transfiguring nobility of the Immolation. That incandesence, and Furtwängler's command of Wagner's *unendliche Melodie*, is heard at its most obvious and potent throughout the first act and final scene of *Walküre*. They are enhanced by the refulgent sound he could draw from any orchestra. The La Scala players, much more accomplished than their Rome brethren, enable Furtwängler to knit together scenes with unerring breadth at quicker speeds than those in either his Rome performance or his 1936 Bayreuth *Ring*.

His approach, at once romantic and tragic, elemental and profound, was characterized thus by Deryck Cooke in discussing the Rome records: 'His ability to make the music surge, or seethe, or melt, so that one has left the world of semiquavers altogether' – though no one was in fact more adept than this conductor at making Wagner's semiquavers sound – 'and is swept up in a great spiritual experience'. I quote Cooke lest you think I am too glowing in my praise. Here is another, Alec Robertson, actually writing about the 1953 studio *Walküre*: 'He carries all Wagner's directions in his head and visualizes each scene in the composer's terms'.

What is true on those sets is even more so in this opera-house recording. You can hear it in the upsurge of glowing sound after Freia is saved, in the 'sehr ausdrucksvoll' passage which is just that before the Wälsungs arrive in Act 2 of *Walküre*, in the whole of the Waltraute scene in *Götterdämmerung*, and of course in the Funeral March and Immolation that crown the whole edifice magificently, solemnly. Wagner's immense peroration has never been at once so spaciously, so thrillingly realized. In this the conductor inspires Flagstad to her greatest achievement. In any case this set at last preserves her complete Brünnhilde for posterity. Mödl and Varnay may extract more intense responses from the text and so convey more of Brünnhilde's anguish and ecstasy, but neither they nor even Nilsson could equal the vocal amplitude and lyrical beauty of Flagstad's singing enshrined here. It is exemplified in the passage 'Der diese Wonne' in the last scene of *Walküre* and 'O, Siegfried! Dein war ich von je' in the *Siegfried* love duet. On this and other evidence. Furtwängler was able to draw from Flagstad a readier response to words, a more subtly expressive manner of phrasing than others.

Most of the other roles are here taken by German-speaking singers, which leads to the inestimable advantage of clear, idiomatic enunciation. But there is more to it than that. Most of the artists were admired by the conductor, who obviously admired singers who relished their words and particularly their consonants. In *Rheingold*, for instance, the veteran Joachim Sattler, whose career stretched back well before the war, has not the most ingratiating voice, but his intelligent, accurate delivery precisely fits the description of Loge as the *Ring's* sole intellectual. Those used to Neidlinger's dominating Alberich may be disconcerted by Pernerstorfer's less powerful portrayal, but again he sings the notes as written without anything of the Bayreuth bark to his delivery. Elisabeth Höngen, not the steadiest of Frickas, is a model of clear utterance, moving too at 'Wotan Gemahl'. Ludwig Weber is another singer who cossets his words and colours his tone in presenting a sympathetic Fasolt. Ferdinand Frantz's Wotan, prosaic on the Rome set, is here enlivened by being heard, as it were, in the theatre. In a sense the whole cast support what is happening in the orchestra; the piercing semiquavers as the gold is stolen, the significant solemnity of the horns, English and French, as love is abjured, the bleak thundering of the Giants' motif, the strings' expansion in Loge's pictorial narration, the sheer evil energy of Alberich's exultation in the third scene.

In *Walküre*, Günther Treptow is almost the Siegmund of one's dreams, a really lyrical *Heldentenor* who also possesses an intelligent mind and an inspired soul so that he is forgiven one or two fluffs as he gets carried away by the excitement of the moment. Hilde Konetzni, in much surer form than three years later, is an eager partner for this Siegmund. The heightened response to the last scene of Act 1 could not possibly be kindled in the studio. Act 2 is less remarkable (Wotan's narration also has a sizeable cut), a moving *Todesverkündigung* from two great singers apart, but in Act 3 a whizzing Ride leads into a splendid final scene, furious Wotan being turned to love by Flagstad's eloquence – and who would not be?

Siegfried was not supposed to be Furtwängler's opera, but here he does marvels with all the voices-of-nature music and with the driving energy of the forging music. The recollection of the Wälsungs' woe in Act 1 could hardly be more moving, the closing duet more ecstatic. The Siegfried is the youthful-sounding, heroic Set Svanholm, so poetic in the Forest Murmurs. Inevitably he tires somewhat towards the end of the long role. Peter Markworth is not such an accurate or precise Mime as Julius Patzak, who sings in the Rome set, but his deft characterization avoids Stolze's exaggerations. Josef Herrmann, a *Heldenbariton* I much admire, is impressive not only for his authentic, unforced tone but also for his legato and superb diction. Höngen's Erda is a considerable achievement, but her best performance in the cycle comes as Waltraute in

Götterdämmerung, remarkable for its urgency and grave tones.

This final opera is distinguished by Max Lorenz's eager, young-sounding (remarkable when you consider he was almost fifty at the time) Siegfried. There are pages when he is too free with his music, but the touch of wonder in his third-act narrative is not be found elsewhere in the complete sets. Weber's plausible, but roughly sung Hagen, Herrmann's virile Gunther (is he too good for the part?), Konetzni's comely Gutrune and more-than-adequate Norns second Flagstad's glorious Brünnhilde. The men of the Scala Chorus suggest raw energy without resorting to coarseness.

The Rome reading is a lesser achievement only when set beside the Scala one; in essence all the positive Furtwängler qualities are to be heard without the full intensity of the opera-house experience, but again there is no doubt that one of the world's great epics is being unfolded before us in a broad yet vigorous performance. Many of the cast are the same as in the Scala-Furtwängler or in other versions, but there are some notable assumptions not yet mentioned or yet encountered, not least Sena Jurinac's lovely Woglinde, and Gutrune and Third Norn, Suthaus's vivid and fine-sounding Siegfried, Rita Streich's ideal Woodbird. Patzak's Mime, as I have already implied, is the work of a scrupulously musical artist – for once sung as Wagner wrote it and the effect is arresting. Alfred Poell is, like Herrmann, an upright Gunther. Margarete Klose, another favourite of this conductor, is a worried Waltraute partnered by Martha Mödl's Brünnhilde, whose committed interpretation, warm, womanly portrayal and uncanny way of judging the precise colouring of words and tone – try 'Ruhe du Gott' – are singular to her.

She connects us with the 1953 Keilberth recording, where she is perhaps even more searching. I do not propose discussing this set in detail; it has never had more than a very limited circulation (one of the singers forced Allegro to withdraw it) and, in any case, it is surpassed in different respects by one or other of the remaining issues. However, I should note Erich

Witte's pointed Loge, Uhde's doubling of Donner and Gunther (one artist sang both parts in the first-ever cycle), Hotter's Wotan in splendid form (and here partnered for the only time on disc by Mödl in *Walküre*, a rewarding combination), and Keilberth's generally straightforward, convincing interpretation. Windgassen's Siegfried is not as full of character as it was to become.

No, if you cannot tolerate the bad sound in Furtwängler's Scala performance or the indifferent acoustic (and poor playing of the orchestra) in the Rome set, you may want to turn to the Goodhall/ENO set. Here, as I have suggested, we have the ensemble performance incarnate under the direction of a true Wagnerian. No matter that he adds some ten minutes to the timing of each act as compared with the slowest Bayreuth conductor; he justifies the breadth of his approach, particularly in the closing work of the tetralogy, by the tragic grandeur and long-drawn phraseology, a total view of the drama that does not exclude care for the *Hauptstimmen* and for instrumental detail. The growth is organic and natural, its effect cumulative. It does not carry you forward irresistibly, inevitably, as does Furtwängler's, but at the end of the journey there is no doubt that the experience has been worthy of the concept.

His singers, as is generally known, studied their roles in the most meticulous and arduous manner with Goodall, thus enabling them to phrase in the broad way he requires and at the same time encompassing Andrew Porter's lucid translation, so faithfully wedded to Wagner's notes and, where possible, to the verbal emphasis of the German. His cast is headed by Rita Hunter's gleaming yet expressive Brünnhilde sung with unflagging consistency of tone and sensitivity, down to the exact execution of the *gruppetti* in the prologue to *Twilight of the Gods*, as it should be called in this context. Indeed it is in that opera that the heroic proportions of her reading can best be heard: in the two preceding operas she seems just marginally less individual and assured in her portrayal.

In the last two operas she is partnered as ever by Alberto

Remedios's fresh, eager Siegfried. Others have made individual episodes more memorable, produced a more full-blooded tone (Melchior certainly), but Remedios's achievement, above all his innate musicality, assure him of a place among the great ones. Norman Bailey's Wotan shows a similar consistency and understanding, only some grittiness in his tone and an occasional reserve of emotion detracting from whole-hearted enjoyment of an articulate assumption. Derek Hammond-Stroud's biting, keenly enunciated Alberich, Emile Belcourt's subtle, witty Loge, Katherine Pring's able Fricka adorn *Rheingold. The Valkyrie* sees Remedios as a lyrical Siegmund and Margaret Curphey as an involved Sieglinde, but here, as in the first act of *Siegfried* (where Gregory Dempsey's Mime conveys character without caricature), there is want of energy, a forward-moving pulse that is inclined to vitiate the physical energy and fire Wagner surely wanted. The bass roles are all well taken, but it would be idle to deny, and chauvinistic to suggest, that for all its welcome ensemble quality, these performances are at all points the answer to a Wagnerian's dream that they have been considered in some quarters. In a highly competitive field, its merits fall into perspective. They *are* remarkable but not unique.

DAS RHEINGOLD

W Wotan; *D* Donner; *F* Frof; *L* Loge; *A* Alberich; *M* Mime; *Fas* Fasolt; *Faf* Fafner; *Fr* Fricka; *E* Erda

1950
(live performance, La Scala, Milan)
Franz *W*; Mattiello *D*; Treptow *F*;
Sattler *L*; Pernerstorfer *A*;
Markworth *M*; Weber *Fas*;
Emmerich *Faf*; Höngen *Fr*;
Weth-Falka *E*/La Scala
Orch./Furtwängler Murray Hill ⓜ
940 477; Everest ⓒ 473/2

1953
(live performance, Bayreuth
Festival) Hotter *W*; Uhde *D*; Stolze
F; Witte *L*; Neidlinger *A*; Kuen *M*;
Weber *Fas*; Greinfl *Faf*; Malaniuk
Fr; von Ilosvay *E*/Bayreuth Festival
Orch./Keilberth Allegro-Elite ⓜ
3125–7

1953
(broadcast performance) Frantz *W*;
Poell *D*; Fehenberger *F*; Windgassen
L; Neidlinger *A*; Patzak *M*; Greindl
Fas; Frick *Faf*; Malaniuk *Fr*;
Siewert *E*/Rome Radio Orch./
Furtwängler EMI ⓜ RLS 706;
Seraphim ⓜ IC 3076

1957
(live performance, Bayreuth
Festival) Hotter *W*; Blankenhein *D*;
Traxel *F*; Suthaus *L*; Neidlinger *A*;
Kuen *M*; van Mill *Fas*; Greindl *Faf*;
von Milinkovic *Fr*; von Ilosvay
E/Bayreuth Festival
Orch./Knappertsbusch Centra ⓜ
LO 50/3

1958
London *W*; Wächter *D*; Kmentt *F*;
Svanholm *L*; Neidlinger *A*; Kuen

M; Kreppel *Fas*; Böhme *Faf*;
Flagstad *Fr*; Madeira *E*/VPO/Solti
Decca SET 382–4 ④ K;
D100D19; London OSA 1309 ④
5–1309

1966
(live performance, Bayreuth
Festival) Adam *W*; Nienstedt *D*;
Esser *F*; Windgassen *L*; Neidlinger
A; Woflfahrt *M*; Talvela *Fas*;
Böhme *Faf*; Burmeister *Fr*;
Soukoupová *E*/Bayreuth Festival
Orch./Böhm Philips 6747 037

1967
Fischer-Dieskau *W*; Kerns *D*; Grobe
F; Stolze *L*; Kélémen *A*; Wohlfahrt
M; Talvela *Fas*; Riddersbusch *Faf*;
Veasey *Fr*; Dominguez *E*/Berlin
PO/Karajan DG 2740 145 ④ 3378
048/9

1968
Polke *W*; Knoll *D*; Doussant *F*; Uhl
L; Kline *A*; H. Kraus *M*; Von Rohr
Fas; Okamura *Faf*; Hesse *Fr*; Boese
E/South German PO/Swarowsky
Westminster WGSO 8175/3

1974
(in English – live performance,
Coliseum, London) Bailey *W*;
Welsby *D*; Ferguson *F*; Belcourt *L*;
Hammond-Stroud *A*; Dempsey *M*;
Lloyd *Fas*; Grant *Faf*; Pring *Fr*;
Collins *E*/English National Opera
Orch./Goodall HMV SLS 5032 ④
TC-SLS 5032, SLS 5146 ④ TC-SLS
5146; Angel SDL 3825Q

DIE WALKÜRE

W Wotan; *S* Siegmund; *Si* Sieglinde; *H* Hunding; *F* Fricka; *B* Brünnhilde

1950
(live performance, La Scala, Milan),
Frantz *W*; Treptow *S*; H Konetzni
Si; Weber *H*; Höngen *F*; Flagstad
B/La Scala Orch./Furtwängler
Murray Hill ⓜ 940 477; Everest ⓔ
474/3

1953
(live performance, Bayreuth
Festival) Hotter *W*; Vinay *S*; Resnik
Si; Greindl *H*; Malaniuk *F*; Mödl
B/Bayreuth Festival
Orch./Keilberth Allegro-Elite ⓜ
3128–32

1953
(broadcast performance) Frantz *W*;
Windgassen *S*; H. Konetzni *Si*; Frick
H; Cavelti *F*; Mödl *B*/Rome Radio
Orch./Furtwängler EMI ⓜ RLS
702; Seraphim ⓜ IE 6077

1954
Frantz *W*; Suthaus *S*; Rysanek *Si*;
Frick *H*; Klöse *F*; Mödl
B/VPO/Furtwängler EMI ⓜ HQM
1019–23; Seraphim ⓜ IE 6012

1957
(live performance, Bayreuth
Festival) Hotter *W*; Vinay *S*;
Nilsson *Si*; Greindl *H*; von
Milinkovic *F*; Varnay *B*/Bayreuth
Festival Orch./Knappertsbusch
Cetra ⓜ LO 59/5

1961
London *W*; Vickers *S*;
Brouwenstijn *Si*; Ward *H*; Gorr *F*;

Nilsson *B*/LSO/Leinsdorf Decca
7BB 125–9; London OSA 1511

1966
Hotter *W*; King *S*; Crespin *Si*; Frick
H; Ludwig *F*; Nilsson *B*/VPO/Solti
Decca SET 312–6 ④ K3W30,
D100D19; London OSA 1509 ④
5–1509

1966
Stewart *W*; Vickers *S*; Janowitz *Si*;
Talvela *H*; Veasey *F*; Crespin
B/Berlin PO/Karajan DG 2740 146
④ 3378 048/9

1967
(live performance, Bayreuth
Festival) Adam *W*; King *S*; Rysanek
Si; Nienstedt *H*; Burmeister *F*;
Nilsson *B*/Bayreuth Festival
Orch./Böhm Philips 6747 037

1968
Polke *W*; McKee *S*; Sommer *Si*; von
Rohr *H*; Hesse *F*; Kniplová *B*/South
German PO/Swarowsky
Westminster WGSO 8176/5

1973
(in English – live performance,
Coliseum, London) Bailey *W*;
Remedios *S*; Curphey *Si*; Grant *H*;
Howard *F*; Hunter *B*/English
National Opera Orch./Goodall
HMV SLS 5063 ④ TC-SLS 5063,
SLS 5146 ④ TC-SLS 5146; Angel
SELX 3826 (Q)

SIEGFRIED

S Siegfried; *M* Mime; *W* Wanderer; *A* Alberich; *F* Fafner; *E* Erda; *B* Brünnhilde; *W* Woodbird

1950
(live performance, La Scala, Milan)
Svanholm *S*; Markworth *M*;
Herrmann *W*; Pernerstorfer *A*;
Weber *F*; Höngen *E*; Flagstad *B*;
Moor *W*/La Scala
Orch./Furtwängler Murray Hill ⓜ
940 477; Everest ⓒ 475/3

1953
(live performance, Bayreuth
Festival) Windgassen *S*; Kuen *M*;
Hotter *S*; Neidlinger *A*; Greindl *F*;
von Ilosvay *E*; Mödl *B*; Streich
W/Bayreuth Festival
Orch./Keilberth Allegro-Elite ⓜ
3133-7

1953
(broadcast performance) Suthaus *S*;
Patzak *M*; Frantz *W*; Pernerstorfer
A; Greindl *F*; Klöse *E*; Mödl *B*;
Streich *W*/Rome Radio
Orch./Furtwängler EMI ⓜ RLS
702; Seraphim ⓜ IE 6078

1957
(live performance, Bayreuth
Festival) Aldenhoff *S*; Kuen *M*;
Hotter *W*; Neidlinger *A*; Greindl *F*;
von Ilosvay *E*; Varnay *B*; Hollweg
W/Bayreuth Festival
Orch./Knappertsbusch Cetra ⓒ
LO 60/5

1962
Windgassen *S*; Stolze *M*; Hotter *W*;
Neidlinger *A*; Böhme *F*; Höffgen *E*;

Nilsson *B*; Sutherland *W*/VPO/Solti
Decca SET 242-6 ④ K, D100D19;
London OSA 1508 ④ 5-1508

1966
(live performance, Bayreuth
Festival) Windgassen *S*; Wohlfhart
M; Adam *W*; Neidlinger *A*; Böhme
F; Soukoupová *E*; Nilsson *B*; Köth
W/Bayreuth Festival Orch./Böhm
Philips 6747 037

1968
McKee *S*; H Hraus *M*; Polke *W*;
Kühne *A*; Okamura *F*; Boese *E*;
Kniplová *B*; Jasper *W*/South
German PO/Swarowsky
Westminster WGSO 8177/5

1968-9
Thomas *S*; Stolze *M*; Stewart *W*;
Kélémen *A*; Riddersbusch *F*;
Dominguez *E*; Dernesch *B*; Gayer
W/Berlin PO/Karajan DG 2740
147 ④ 3378 048/9

1973
(in English – live performance,
Coliseum London) Remedios *S*;
Dempsey *M*; Bailey *W*;
Hammond-Stroud *A*; Grant *F*;
Collins *E*; Hunter *B*; M. London
W/Sadler's Wells Opera
Orch./Goodall HMV SLS 875 ④
TC-SLS 875, SLS 5146 ④ TC-SLS
5146

GÖTTERDÄMMERUNG

B Brünnhilde; *S* Siegfried; *G* Gunther; *A* Alberich; *H* Hagen; *Gut* Gutrune

1950
(live performance, La Scala, Milan)
Flagstad *B*; Lorenz *S*; Herrmann *G*;
Pernerstofer *A*; Weber *H*; H.
Konetzni *Gut*/La Scala
Orch./Furtwängler Murray Hill ⓜ
940 477; Everest ⓔ 476/3

1953
(live performance, Bayreuth
Festival) Mödl *B*; Windgassen *S*;
Udhe *G*; Neidlinger *A*; Greindl *H*;
Hinsch-Gröndal *Gut*/Bayreuth
Festival Chorus and
Orch./Keilberth Allegro-Elite ⓜ
3138–42

1953
(broadcast performance) Mödl *B*;
Sauthaus *S*; Poell *G*; Pernerstorfer
A; Greindl *H*; Jurinac *Gut*/Rome
Radio Chorus and
Orch./Furtwängler EMI ⓜ RLS
702; Seraphim ⓜ IE 6079

1955
Flagstad *B*; Svanholm *S*; Johnsen *G*;
Gronneberg *A*; Norfsjö *H*; Bjöner
Gut/Oslo Opera Chorus,
Norwegian Radio Chorus, Oslo
PO/Fjelstad Decca ⓜ LXT
5205–10; London ⓜ OSA 52438

1957
(live performance, Bayreuth
Festival) Varnay *B*; Windgassen *S*;
Uhde *G*; Neidlinger *H*; Grünner
Gut/Bayreuth Festival Chorus and
Orch./Knappertsbusch Cetra ⓜ
LO 61/5

1964
Nilsson *B*; Windgassen *S*;
Fischer-Dieskau *G*; Neidlinger *A*;
Frick *H*; Watson *Gut*/Vienna State
Opera Chorus, VPO/Solti Decca
SET 292–7 ④ K; D100D19;
London OSA ④ 5–1604

1967
(live performance, Bayreuth
Festival) Nilsson *B*; Windgassen *S*;
Stewart *G*; Neidlinger *A*; Greindl *H*;
Dvořáková *Gut*/Bayreuth Chorus
and Orch./Böhm Philips 6747 037

1968
kniplová *B*; McKee *S*; Knoll *G*;
Kühne *A*; van Rohr *H*; Sommer
Gut/Vienna State Opera Chorus,
South German PO/Swarowsky
Westminster WGSO 8178/6

1969–70
Dernesch *B*; Brilioth *S*; Stewart *G*;
Kélémen *A*; Ridderbusch *H*;
Janowitz *Gut*/German Opera
Chorus Berlin PO/Karajan DG 2740
148 ④ 3378 048/9

1977
(in English – live performance,
Coliseum, London) Hunter *B*;
Remedios *S*; Welsby *G*; Hammond
Stroud *A*; Haugland *H*; Curphey
Gut/English National Opera
Chorus and Orch./Goodall HMV
SLS 5118 ④ TC-SLS 5118; SLS
5146 ④ TC-SLS 5146